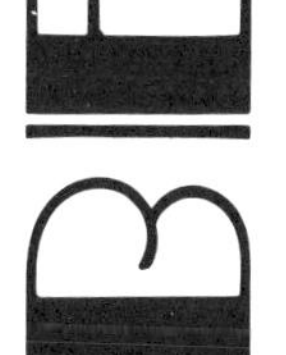

BEGINNING LIGHT

from the editors of

**IN THE BEGINNING
& BEGINNING AGAIN**

**mouthwatering low fat, low cholesterol
hors d'oeuvres and soup recipes
- - -for heart smart cooks- - -**

Cover design by Alice H. Balterman

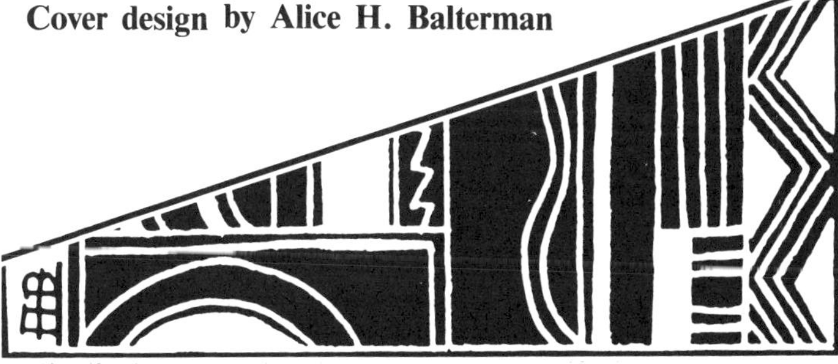

**rockdale ridge press
8501 ridge road
cincinnati, ohio, 45236
513-891-9900**

1st Printing — December, 1990

BEGINNING LIGHT

ISBN 0-9602338-6-5

Library of Congress Cataloging in Publication Data

Main Entry Under Title:

BEGINNING LIGHT

Includes Index.
Cookery (low fat, low cholesterol appetizers and soups)

TX740.15   641.8'12   90-092174

Printed by
The Feicke Printing Co.
Cincinnati, Ohio

Typography by
Reporter Typographics
Cincinnati, Ohio

EDITORIAL AND PRODUCTION STAFF

Editors
Sue Richard
Barbara Rosenberg

Cover Art
Alice Balterman

Book Design
Marilyn Asch
Jackie Lindauer

Editorial Writing
Sally Korkin
Millie Tieger

Word Processing
Doris Berman
Etheljane Callner

Nutritive Analysis
Ann Arnoff
Ellen Kleinfeld, R.D., L.D
Susan Tillipman

Proof Readers
Linda Abrahamson
Peggy Barrett
Dottie Eichel
Nancy Friedman
Barbara Glas

Index
Ellen Dunsker
Peggy Selonick

Librarian
Joan Schaengold

Legal
Marianne Mandell-Brown

Accounting
Fredda Leitman
Sylvia Rosenthaler

Mailing
Bernice Nelson

Recipe Development
Linda Abrahamson
Bryna Altbaier
Ellie Bissinger
Elaine Bloom
Rosemary Bloom
Ellen Buchsbaum
Barbara Cohen
Cathy Frisch
Bercie Frohman
Cynthia Frohman
Harriet Feigenblatt
Dr. Meryl Goldman
Diana Goodman
Judy Green
Jim Gregory
Audrey Gutmann
Marj Heilbrun
Marilyn Hirschhorn
Hildy Kerman
Deanie Kolstein
Helene Mack
Rosella Mathieu
Raphael Moreno
Phyllis Ringel
Barbara Reed
Abbie Schwartz
Sally Schwartz
Lenore Stulbarg
Iris Werthaiser
Betty Ann Wolf

BEGINNING LIGHT has been a team effort. The individual and collective dedication of this committee has provided continuing inspiration.

FOREWORD

BEGINNING LIGHT is dedicated to hosts and hostesses everywhere who search for a cookbook of healthful, elegant, easy to prepare hors d'oeuvres. We have developed this collection of mouth watering recipes to meet today's direction toward heart healthful, low fat, low cholesterol fare.

The goal of **BEGINNING LIGHT** is to offer you, the chef, specialized recipes for the preparation of delicious hors d'oeuvres and soups for party entertaining and family dining. We eliminate hidden fat and cholesterol with careful substitutions and innovations. New recipes and adaptations of all time favorites combine to present to today's cook easy to prepare, attractive and, most importantly, health conscious delights.

Thoughtful and creative cooks have contributed to **BEGINNING LIGHT.** As you add **BEGINNING LIGHT** to your cookbook collection, you may be assured that the most precise, scientific and skilled information, garnered from dieticians, chefs, cooks, and research teams, has been combined into delicious, tantalizing, heart and health aware hors d'oeuvres.

Enjoy **BEGINNING LIGHT.** Your family and your guests will sing your praises for their gustatory pleasure and for their healthful future.

CONTENTS

ILLUMINATING BEGINNING LIGHT

WHY DO DINERS LOVE HORS D'OEUVRES?

Before a meal, hors d'oeuvres give a real and emotional boost to the hungry diner. They are the appetite pleasers that offer gratification to the palate in a friendly setting. Often, alcohol and other beverages dull the taste buds, calling for highly seasoned hors d'oeuvres as accompaniments. **BEGINNING LIGHT** presents recipes that offer moderation without deprivation. The big taste is there, in health conscious recipes offering fat and cholesterol sparing flavors that we crave.

SPOTLIGHT

Throughout **BEGINNING LIGHT,** there are a number of special notes starting with the word **SPOTLIGHT.** Each **SPOTLIGHT** contains information that will assist you in becoming a skilled and savvy, knowledgeable chef who can cook up a storm with guidance from **SPOTLIGHT'S** bright ideas as your lighthouse.

LEARN LIGHT AND LIVE

In the center of **BEGINNING LIGHT** (LEARN LIGHT AND LIVE, Chapter 6), you'll find comparison charts designed to heighten your awareness of what you are eating now and what you can accomplish with healthier yet still appetizing options. Additionally you will find substitutions, label reading, and shopping tips on how to keep recipes low in fat and cholesterol. A black triangle at the top corner of each page points out important information.

HEART SMART

Heartsmart recipes
and techniques are
noted with a ♡ and
are the particular favorites
of the editors.
They can't
be beat!

NOTES ON NUTRITIVE ANALYSIS

FOR RECIPES CONTAINING MARINADES:

Nutrient analyses relating to the amount of salt, sugar or oil contained within the marinade is lower than that depicted. Since most of the marinade is discarded, only a portion of these nutrients is ingested.

FOR RECIPES CONTAINING ALCOHOL:

Although alcohol evaporates when heated, there is controversy regarding the extent of evaporation. Accordingly, we have calculated the nutritional values based on the actual quantity of alcohol used, taking no evaporation into account. Consequently, the *calorie* and *carbohydrate* content will be significantly lower than stated.

CONCERNING OUR NUTRITIVE VALUES:

Where there is a variance in the stated quantity of an ingredient, the nutritive value has been calculated with the lower amount.

Nutritive values do not include optional ingredients.

IN ABSENCE OF NUTRIENT VALUE CHART:

The nutrient analysis of some recipes could not be computed due to the variance in size of a product and/or to the nonuniformity in techniques or skills of the cook.

FOR YOUR INFORMATION

This cookbook contains recipes that have been screened carefully to be of low fat and low cholesterol content. The recipes also provide the user with helpful hints to reduce the salt content. However, **BEGINNING LIGHT** in no way represents itself to be a salt-free cookbook. Those individuals requiring a restricted diet of any kind are advised to seek the advice of their physician or dietician concerning each recipe and its ingredients.

The authors/publishers recognize that the responsibility of restricted diet care lies with the individual and therefore assume no liability.

The Diet Simple Plus™ *Program,* a computer software program, was used to calculate most nutritional values. For those ingredients not available in the data base, the dietary information was derived from the *Nutritive Value of American Foods* or was provided by the manufacturers of the specific products. All nutrient analysis is based on the most current data available at time of publication.

1
CHICKEN, TURKEY
and a bit of meat

BASIC GROUND POULTRY MIX

Once you've tried ground poultry, you'll have a hard time being faithful to old ground beef habits. Many dishes traditionally made with ground beef may be made successfully with ground poultry. There is a wide variation in percentages of fat in packaged ground poultry. Be aware that the packaged products may contain some high fat, high cholesterol portions of skin. READ THE LABELS! You may choose to grind the meat at home or have your butcher remove all visible fat before he grinds it for you.

Treat yourself to ground chicken breast for a more delicate flavor and texture.

*1	pound ground turkey or chicken, breast or thigh	1 teaspoon dehydrated onion (optional)
1	egg white	**1/3 cup bread crumbs
1	tablespoon vegetable oil	1/4 teaspoon pepper
1/4	teaspoon salt	A pinch of freshly ground nutmeg (optional)

Mix gently to blend. Proceed with recipe.

*GROUND POULTRY vs. BEEF COMPARISON CHART (Page 139)

**For Italian dishes use Italian flavored bread crumbs.

The nutritive analyses of recipes using this poultry mix were evaluated using raw ground turkey.

YIELD: 30 meatballs

Nutritive Values (per piece)		calories	31.0 kc
total fat	1.8 g	carbohydrates	0.8 g
monosaturated fat	0.6 g	fiber	0.0 g
polyunsaturated fat	0.6 g	protein	2.9 g
saturated fat	0.5 g	sodium	39.7 mg
cholesterol	11.2 mg	sugar	0.1 g

CHICKEN PICCATA

If you like it more tart use the larger amount of lemon juice and pucker up.

1   recipe BASIC GROUND POULTRY MIX (Page 17), shaped into 24 balls
2   teaspoons margarine
1   cup dry white wine
1/3-1/2 cup lemon juice, freshly squeezed
2   tablespoons capers
2   teaspoons Parmesan cheese, freshly grated
         *Instant blend flour to thicken

**1. Sauté shaped chicken balls in margarine in nonstick skillet, just long enough to brown on all sides.

2. Add wine and lemon juice to skillet. Bring to boil. Simmer for 10 minutes, turning once to coat with sauce.

3. Add capers and Parmesan cheese, stirring carefully to avoid breaking balls.

4. Thicken pan juices with instant blend flour, using enough to thicken.

*SPOTLIGHT (Page 94)

**A teflon electric skillet is ideal.

SPOTLIGHT *sizzles in a nonstick electric skillet which offers a method of cooking with little or no fat. Food may be prepared ahead and reheated or may be made at the table.*

YIELD: 24 meatballs			
Nutritive Values (per piece)		calories	51.0 kc
total fat	2.7 g	carbohydrates	1.5 g
monosaturated fat	0.9 g	fiber	trace
polyunsaturated fat	1.0 g	protein	3.7 g
saturated fat	0.7 g	sodium	77.6 mg
cholesterol	14.0 mg	sugar	0.2 g

♥ CHICKEN MATZO BALLS

They look like matzo balls, but wait till you taste them!

²/₃	cup matzo meal	3	egg whites
3	tablespoons vegetable oil	1	tablespoon chopped parsley (1 teaspoon dried)
¼	cup water	1	pound raw ground chicken breast, fat removed
¼	teaspoon salt Few grinds pepper		

1. Combine first 7 ingredients; add ground chicken, mixing well to blend.

2. Shape into 18-30 balls according to how you plan to use them. Drop into 3 quarts boiling water. Return water to boil; reduce heat and simmer covered for 15 minutes.

Add to your favorite soup for a hearty starter.

YIELD: 30 balls

Nutritive Values (per ball)		calories	42.0 kc
total fat	1.6 g	carbohydrates	2.5 g
monosaturated fat	0.3 g	fiber	0.1 g
polyunsaturated fat	0.9 g	protein	4.1 g
saturated fat	0.2 g	sodium	33.2 mg
cholesterol	8.8 mg	sugar	trace g

MINIATURE STUFFED CABBAGES

2	small cabbages	½	cup white raisins
1	cup chopped onion	1	cup cooked rice (⅓ cup raw)
1	clove garlic, sliced		
2	15-ounce cans tomato sauce	1½	pounds ground chicken or turkey
1	tablespoon margarine	¼	cup grated onion
2	cups water	¼-½	teaspoon salt
	Juice of 3 lemons	⅛	teaspoon pepper
⅔	cup brown sugar, tightly packed	½	cup ginger snaps, crumbled

1. Select small firm cabbages and boil until leaves become flexible enough to separate and roll (about 5 minutes). Set aside to cool.

2. In a large nonstick skillet sauté onions and garlic in margarine. Add tomato sauce, water, lemon juice, brown sugar, and raisins. Simmer for 15 minutes.

3. Add raw ground chicken or turkey to cooked rice; add grated onion, salt and pepper to raw meat mixture.

4. Separate cabbage leaves. Trim the base of the leaf with vegetable peeler to the same thickness as rest of leaf.

5. Roll meat-rice mixture (approximately 2 tablespoons) into cabbage leaves. Secure with good quality wood toothpicks.

MINIATURE STUFFED CABBAGES *(continued)*

6. Place carefully into tomato sauce mixture and cook slowly for 1 hour, covered.

7. Mix ginger snaps with ¾ cup sauce. Add to remaining sauce during last 10 minutes. Stir occasionally to prevent burning or sticking.

These meat balls are also very good without the cabbage wrap.

Better made one day ahead and refrigerated overnight. Can be reheated in casserole dish in oven.

SPOTLIGHT *is on hors d'oeuvres wrapped in vegetable leaves. This is an exciting cross cultural method of using healthful ingredients in a healthful wrap utilizing spinach, cabbage, lettuce or grape leaves. The cook will be wrapped in praise when serving low fat, high fiber hors d'oeuvres. Turn over a new leaf.*

YIELD: 30 pieces

Nutritive Values (per piece)		calories	112.0 kc
total fat	3.4 g	carbohydrates	16.6 g
monosaturated fat	0.9 g	fiber	1.7 g
polyunsaturated fat	0.8 g	protein	5.3 g
saturated fat	0.8 g	sodium	264.0 mg
cholesterol	16.7 mg	sugar	8.8 g

COCKTAIL BALLS

MEATBALLS:

2   recipes BASIC GROUND POULTRY MIX (Page 17)

SAUCE:

8   ounces grape jelly
¾   cup water

1   bottle chili sauce
3   tablespoons lemon juice

ALTERNATE SAUCE:

1   10-ounce jar apricot preserves
¼   cup "hot" barbecue sauce

3   tablespoons lemon juice
½   cup water

1. Shape meatballs. Chill at least 1 hour.

2. Combine sauce ingredients and simmer 30 minutes.

3. Add meatballs to sauce. Heat sauce to boiling and simmer for 20 minutes.

Make ahead and freeze. Reheat when ready to serve.

To reduce sodium use low sodium chili sauce and salt substitute.

YIELD: 60 balls

Nutritive Values (per ball)		calories	46.4 kc
total fat	1.8 g	carbohydrates	4.6 g
monosaturated fat	0.6 g	fiber	trace
polyunsaturated fat	0.6 g	protein	2.9 g
saturated fat	0.5 g	sodium	92.0 mg
cholesterol	11.6 g	sugar	1.9 g

BARBECUED CHICKEN BALLS

⅔ cup barbecue sauce
1   recipe BASIC POULTRY MIX (Page 17)

1. Pour ⅓ cup barbecue sauce in a bake and serve dish.

2. Shape meat into 1-inch balls. Place in prepared dish; top with remaining sauce.

3. Bake in pre-heated 350° oven for 20 minutes, basting once with sauce.

Serve with toothpicks or plates and forks.

YIELD: 30 meatballs

Nutritive Values (per piece)		calories	36.0 kc
total fat	1.9 g	carbohydrates	1.5 g
monosaturated fat	0.7 g	fiber	trace
polyunsaturated fat	0.7 g	protein	2.9 g
saturated fat	0.5 g	sodium	8.5 mg
cholesterol	11.2 mg	sugar	0.7 g

SWEET AND SOUR MEATBALLS

A great do it ahead recipe!

1 recipe BASIC GROUND POULTRY MIX (Page 17)	1 tablespoon oil
3 tablespoons cornstarch	1½ cups pineapple juice
1 tablespoon soy sauce	1 20-ounce can crushed pineapple, drained (save juice)
3 tablespoons vinegar	1 green pepper, diced
⅓ cup sugar	1 jar sliced pimiento, drained

1. Form poultry mix into 30 small balls. Bake at 375° on lightly greased pan for 10 minutes, uncovered.

2. Mix cornstarch with soy sauce, vinegar, ¼ cup pineapple juice and sugar. Blend well to remove lumps. Add oil and remaining pineapple juice. Bring to boil, stirring frequently and cook 1 minute until thickened.

3. Add green pepper to sauce with pineapple.

4. Add meatballs. Heat until meatballs are warmed through.

Meatballs may be baked and frozen ahead. Sauce may be made ahead, but add pineapple, green pepper and pimiento at time of reheating. Serve piping hot.

As a main course, add ½ cup sliced water chestnuts and 1 cup pea pods. Serve over rice. Meatballs may be larger in size.

To reduce sodium content, use lite soy sauce and salt substitute.

YIELD: 30 meatballs

Nutritive Values (per piece)		calories	60.0 kc
total fat	2.3 g	carbohydrates	7.2 g
monosaturated fat	1.0 g	fiber	0.2 g
polyunsaturated fat	0.7 g	protein	3.1 g
saturated fat	0.6 g	sodium	74.5 mg
cholesterol	11.2 mg	sugar	4.9 g

DAH BIN LO

A congenial "do-it at the table" first course. Serve with a nice Chinese Plum Wine. When everyone has finished cooking, serve the deliciously flavored hot broth in cups.

6 cups CHICKEN BROTH (Page 208) or canned
1 tablespoon chopped parsley
Chicken breast cut into 1-inch pieces
Whole fresh mushrooms

Tofu (extra firm) cut into 1-inch squares
Raw shrimp
Fresh sea scallops
2 whole shallots, peeled

As a rule of thumb, plan 8 pieces per person. Select from the listed options according to the rest of your menu. You may have some innovative ideas of your own.

1. Place fondue pot or electric skillet where it is easily accessible, surrounded with bowls of chicken, scallops, tofu, shrimp, and mushrooms. Have chopsticks or fondue forks, bread and butter plates and soup cups available for each guest.

2. Fill pot with 2 inches chicken broth. Bring to boil, add shallots and parsley and simmer for 5 minutes.

3. Each guest selects the items of his choice with chopsticks, places them in boiling broth. After 3 or 4 minutes, guest removes cooked food to plate. Replenish broth as it evaporates.

Serve along with a selection of the following sauces:

Hot mustard sauce

Sweet and sour sauce (the kind used for egg roll)

Teriyaki sauce

Plum sauce

Tartar sauce (for fish)

Béarnaise sauce (make it with margarine and use VERY sparingly)

The remaining soup will be very high in sodium unless you use a low sodium soup to start. Nutritive values depend on your guests' appetites.

DOLMADES

Stuffed grapevine leaves. We have reduced cholesterol and saturated fat by substituting fish and chicken for the traditional lamb.

2 tablespoons olive oil	1 tablespoon fresh lemon juice, reserve rind
½ cup chopped onion or scallion	½ teaspoon salt
1-2 large cloves garlic, chopped	A few grinds of pepper
2 tablespoons pine nuts	3 tablespoons white raisins
1½ cups cooked brown rice	1 tablespoon chopped mint leaves (optional)
½ cup chopped dill weed (2 tablespoons dried)	1 jar grape vine leaves in brine
½ cup chopped parsley (3 tablespoons dried)	Olive oil spray
*1 pound ground raw chicken or ground raw fish (scrod or halibut)	2 cups chicken broth, fat removed
	½ cup dry white wine

1. Sauté onion in olive oil until transparent; add garlic and pine nuts and continue cooking for 2 minutes. *(Do not brown garlic.)*

2. Add next 9 ingredients.

3. Rinse grape leaves to remove excess brine; drain on paper towels. Cut off stems and cut larger leaves in half.

DOLMADES *(continued)*

4. Prepare cooking pot: spray with oil; cover bottom with reserved lemon rind cut into strips and with a layer of grape leaves.

5. Arrange remaining grape leaves on work surface. Place 1 level tablespoon of filling in center of each grape leaf. Fold over top and sides like an envelope and roll.

6. Arrange in layers in pot, seam side down. Add chicken broth and wine. Weight down with an inverted plate. Bring to boil, cover and simmer for 40 minutes.

Serve with AVGOLEMONO SAUCE (Page 236).

*To grind at home, place in food processor with steel blade. Process with 4-6 on/off pulses.

For a meatless version, omit chicken or fish and increase rice to 2½ cups.

Wilted leaf lettuce leaves can be substituted for grape leaves.

Nutritive values calculated with ground chicken. To reduce sodium use low sodium chicken broth and correct seasoning with salt substitute.

YIELD: 40 pieces

Nutritive Values (per piece)		calories	40.6 kc
total fat	2.0 g	carbohydrates	2.8 g
monosaturated fat	1.0 g	fiber	0.2 g
polyunsaturated fat	0.4 g	protein	2.5 g
saturated fat	0.5 g	sodium	77.7 mg
cholesterol	8.4 mg	sugar	0.5 g

TURKEY STROGANOFF BALLS

An inexpensive version of a gourmet recipe which usually uses steak as the meat. We've reduced fat and cholesterol by substituting lean ground turkey and powdered buttermilk for steak and sour cream.

½ cup chopped onion
½ teaspoon margarine
1 pound ground turkey
1 teaspoon celery salt, divided
¼ teaspoon pepper
½ cup bread crumbs
½ cup water
3 ounces low sodium tomato paste
3 tablespoons bouillon or chicken broth

½ cup sherry
1 tablespoon Worcestershire
¼ cup sliced green pepper
1 tablespoon caraway seeds
*2 tablespoons powdered buttermilk, dissolved in 1 tablespoon water

1. Mix ground turkey, ½ teaspoon celery salt, pepper, bread crumbs, and water. Form into 30 small balls. Bake on greased pan in 500° oven for 6-8 minutes.

2. Sauté onion in margarine in nonstick skillet. Add tomato paste, bouillon, sherry, Worcestershire and remaining celery salt. Simmer 20 minutes.

3. Add caraway seed and green pepper and simmer 10 minutes longer. Stir in buttermilk and heat just to boiling point. Do not boil buttermilk. . . it will curdle.

Prepare in advance through step 2. Freeze or refrigerate 1-3 days. Thaw. Heat to boiling. Resume directions at step 3.

*SPOTLIGHT (Page 93)

To reduce sodium, substitute salt-free herb seasoning for celery salt and use low sodium chicken broth.

YIELD: 30 meatballs			
Nutritive Values (per piece)		calories	37.4 kc
total fat	1.5 g	carbohydrates	2.0 g
monosaturated fat	0.6 g	fiber	0.2 g
polyunsaturated fat	0.8 g	protein	3.1 g
saturated fat	0.5 g	sodium	126.6 mg
cholesterol	11.5 mg	sugar	0.7 g

COOKING CHICKEN BREASTS

POACHING METHOD

For the tenderest chicken breasts try this stovetop method.

6 pounds chicken breasts, skinned	½ cup chopped celery leaves
½ teaspoon salt	2 tablespoons chopped onion

1. Place chicken breasts in pot. Cover with boiling water. Add remaining ingredients. Return to boil. Cover pot.

2. Reduce heat and simmer for 5 minutes.

3. Turn off heat and leave chicken in hot water 15 minutes.

4. Test for doneness by slicing into thickest part. It should not be pink in color.

COOKING BAG METHOD

Quick and easy and no pots to wash!

3-5 pounds chicken breasts, skinned	Seasoned salt
	1 tablespoon flour

1. Preheat oven to 325°.

2. Sprinkle chicken breasts with seasoned salt.

3. Place flour in Reynolds Oven Cooking Bag.

4. Place chicken breasts in bag and place bag in 2-inch deep pan.

5. Close bag with twister and cut six ½-inch slits in top of bag.

6. Bake in preheated oven for 45 minutes.

7. Remove from oven and let stand for 15 minutes.

8. Cut off a corner of bag and drain broth into a jar.

Freeze or refrigerate broth for future use.

JELLIED CHICKEN IN ASPIC

Serve for an hors d'oeuvre or in larger portions at a summer cocktail buffet.

*2   1-pound chicken breasts, skinned and poached
1½ cups concentrated consommé with gelatin added
1   large pimiento, cut into strips
1   7-ounce can hearts of palm, split lengthwise into ¼ inch strips
4   canned artichoke hearts, drained and quartered

1. Cover the bottom of a 12 inch serving platter with half the consommé. Place in freezer until just set, but not frozen.

2. Split chicken breasts and cut into portions to fit slices of party rye. Lay chicken slices neatly into the consommé.

3. Surround chicken in attractive design with pimiento, hearts of palm and artichoke hearts. If consommé has softened, return to refrigerator to set.

4. Pour remaining consommé over chicken and vegetables. Refrigerate until gelatin has set. Cover with plastic wrap and refrigerate several hours or overnight. Accompany with an assortment of the following sauces:

SALMON SAUCE (Page 245)

CUCUMBER DILL SAUCE (Page 243)

MANGO CHUTNEY (Page 237)

PLUM TOMATO SALSA (Page 240)

*COOKING CHICKEN BREASTS (Page 29)

YIELD: 8 servings

Nutritive Values (per serving)		calories	228.0 kc
total fat	85.0 g	carbohydrates	1.8 g
monosaturated fat	3.3 g	fiber	0.4 g
polyunsaturated fat	1.8 g	protein	33.9 g
saturated fat	3.3 g	sodium	189.8 mg
cholesterol	85.6 mg	sugar	0.2 g

GRILLED CURRIED CHICKEN TIDBITS IN ORANGE SAUCE

1 tablespoon Dijon mustard or raspberry mustard	1 teaspoon thyme
⅓ cup frozen orange juice concentrate, undiluted	1 boullion cube
1 tablespoon curry powder	4 whole chicken breasts, skinned, boned and halved, visible fat removed
1 tablespoon dried tarragon	½ cup dry white wine
	*Instant blend flour to thicken

1. Combine first 6 ingredients in a plastic bag. Place chicken in bag. Close bag with twister. Marinate several hours or overnight in refrigerator, turning bag occasionally to coat chicken with marinade.

2. When ready to serve, remove chicken from bag. Drain and place marinade in a small pan with wine.

3. Bring marinade to boiling point; simmer for 5 minutes and stir in instant blend flour to thicken lightly. Set aside.

4. Grill chicken for 5 minutes; turn and continue grilling for 5 minutes longer. (Be sure that the chicken is not pink inside.)

5. Cut chicken into 1 inch cubes and serve with hot thickened marinade for dipping.

Chicken also may be broiled in oven or sautéed in nonstick electric skillet.

This recipe makes a fabulous main course. Give it a try and expect raves.

*SPOTLIGHT (Page 94)

YIELD: 10 servings

Nutritive Values (per serving)		calories	179.6 kc
total fat	2.1 g	carbohydrates	4.0 g
monosaturated fat	0.0 g	fiber	0.3 g
polyunsaturated fat	0.4 g	protein	32.4 g
saturated fat	5.0 g	sodium	194.6 mg
cholesterol	79.0 mg	sugar	0.0 g

TEXAS BARBECUED DRUMETTES

Use your fingers and enjoy!

½ cup barbecue sauce
1 tablespoon dry wine or lemon juice

1 tablespoon chili powder
*18 chicken drumettes, skin removed

1. Mix first three ingredients.

2. Dip drumettes into sauce and place in baking pan. Bake at 375° for 30 minutes, basting occasionally.

This method can also be used with ½ pound of chicken tenders, cut into bite-sized pieces. Bake 15 minutes.

*Perhaps your friend, the butcher, will remove the skin for you!

CUTTING WINGS INTO DRUMETTES

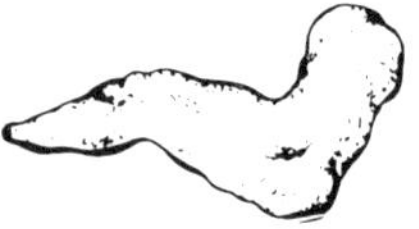

1. Flatten wing on cutting board with wingtip on left and thicker (drumette) portion on right.

2. Cut through joint.

Retain drumette only. Save remaining parts for stock pot.

Pictures courtesy of the National Broiler Council.

YIELD: 18 drumettes			
Nutritive Values (per piece)		calories	42.0 kc
total fat	2.1 g	carbohydrates	1.2 g
monosaturated fat	0.8 g	fiber	0.2 g
polyunsaturated fat	0.5 g	protein	4.7 g
saturated fat	0.5 g	sodium	76.0 mg
cholesterol	16.3 mg	sugar	0.8 g

TURKEY ON A TOOTHPICK

This is a great picnic hors d'oeuvre. Serve with toothpicks.

2	pounds turkey sausage	1	red pepper
2	tablespoons pickling spices		Distilled vinegar

1. Cut sausage into bite-sized cubes.

2. Pack gently into quart jar.

3. Add pickling spices and red pepper.

4. Fill jar with vinegar. Put lid on jar.

5. Refrigerate for 24 hours before using.

SPOTLIGHT *on turkey sausage. While the use of turkey in sausage production has reduced the fat and cholesterol content as much as 25%, sausage is still a high fat food. The fat and cholesterol content will vary according to the formula of the manufacturer. READ THE LABEL!*

SPICY SAUSAGE

*1   1-pound smoked turkey sausage, peeled

2   tablespoons teriyaki sauce

2   teaspoons Worcestershire sauce

2   tablespoons corn syrup or maple syrup

Freshly ground pepper

1. Place peeled sausage in plastic bag with teriyaki and Worcestershire. Marinate several hours, turning occasionally.

2. Bake for 30 minutes at 350°, basting several times with pan drippings.

Slice into 1 inch pieces. Serve on toothpicks with assorted mustards for dipping. Makes 10-12 pieces.

*SPOTLIGHT (Page 33)

VARIATIONS:

Instead of marinating sausage, place in foil lined pan and spread with mixture of:

2 teaspoons Dijon mustard
¼ cup apricot preserves

or

½ cup crushed pineapple
2 teaspoons brown sugar
2 teaspoons Dijon mustard

The nutritive values will vary according to the recipe of the sausage manufacturer.

MELON PROSCIUTTO CUBES

1. Cut cantaloupe or honeydew into 1 inch cubes.

2. Trim visable fat from thinly sliced prosciutto.

3. Wrap a small piece of prosciutto around each cube. Fasten with a toothpick. Serve cold.

ASPARAGUS PROSCIUTTO SPEARS

1. Trim visible fat from thinly sliced prosciutto.

2. Wrap a small piece of prosciutto around a cooked and chilled asparagus spear.

3. Fasten with toothpick. Serve cold.

For an attractive presentation place each ASPARAGUS PROSCIUTTO SPEAR on endive leaf cut to fit.

SPOTLIGHT *contrasts flavors of paper thin prosciutto and sweet melon, salty and sweet, a treat in moderation if salt is restricted.*

Nutritive values for prosciutto hors d'oeuvres will depend upon the thickness of the prosciutto slices.

GARLIC TENDERLOIN SLICES

2   **pounds pork or beef tenderloin, visible fat removed**
⅓   **cup teriyaki sauce**
4   **cloves garlic, halved**

1. Place all ingredients in a plastic bag; fasten with twister. Marinate in refrigerator for 48 hours, turning bag occasionally.

2. To roast, preheat oven to 500°. Remove meat from bag and place on foil lined, oil sprayed roasting pan, doubling narrow end of meat under. Baste meat with marinade. Place in preheated oven and immediately reduce temperature to 300°.

3. Bake pork tenderloin for 1 hour, basting with marinade every 15 minutes. Bake beef tenderloin for 20-25 minutes, or to desired degree of doneness, basting every 8 minutes.

4. Cool before slicing into ⅛ inch slices.

Serve with party rye and assorted mustards.

To reduce sodium, use low sodium terriyaki or soy sauce.

YIELD: 48 ½-ounce slices of Beef

Nutritive Values (per slice)		calories	32.0 kc
total fat	1.5 g	carbohydrates	0.4 g
monosaturated fat	trace	fiber	0.0 g
polyunsaturated fat	0.0 g	protein	4.0 g
saturated fat	0.2 g	sodium	86.5 mg
cholesterol	11.7 mg	sugar	0.0 g

SPOTLIGHT *reminds you that you can "lean" on pork. Trimmed pork tenderloin has the lowest fat and cholesterol count of all the cuts of pork.*

YIELD: 72 ⅓-ounce slices of Pork

Nutritive Values (per slice)		calories	15.4 kc
total fat	0.3 g	carbohydrates	0.3 g
monosaturated fat	trace	fiber	0.0 g
polyunsaturated fat	0.0 g	protein	2.7 g
saturated fat	0.1 g	sodium	57.3 mg
cholesterol	8.2 mg	sugar	0.0 g

GRILLED FLANK STEAK

1	pound flank steak	¾	teaspoon garlic salt
¼	cup oil	3	tablespoons honey
¼	cup soy sauce		Miniature buns or
2	tablespoons vinegar		party rye
1	teaspoon powdered ginger		

1. Remove visible fat from steak. Place steak in plastic bag.

2. Combine next 6 ingredients; pour over steak. Marinate in refrigerator several hours or overnight, turning bag occasionally.

3. Remove steak from marinade.

4. Cook briefly on grill or broil in oven (meat should be rare).

Slice in thin strips, cutting across grain. Serve on miniature buns or party rye.

The fat and sodium content of this recipe will be significantly lower than stated since much of the marinade is discarded. To reduce sodium, substitute low sodium soy sauce and garlic powder.

YIELD: 10 servings

Nutritive Values (per serving)		calories	265.5 kc
total fat	97.0 g	carbohydrates	19.9 g
monosaturated fat	2.5 g	fiber	1.9 g
polyunsaturated fat	1.7 g	protein	16.4 g
saturated fat	0.9 g	sodium	412.0 mg
cholesterol	0.0 mg	sugar	8.1 g

GRILLED BEEF STRIPS

1	pound round steak, about 1 inch thick	1	teaspoon sugar	
1	clove garlic, thinly sliced	⅓	cup soy sauce	
2	tablespoons sherry	1	1-inch piece of fresh ginger, thinly sliced or 1 teaspoon ground ginger	

1. Remove fat from meat and slice very thin. (It is easier to do if meat is partially frozen.)

2. Mix remaining ingredients and marinate meat strips in mixture for at least ½ hour.

3. Thread meat on skewers and broil briefly over hot coals on grill or hibachi.

SPOTLIGHT *on beef: not all beef is high in fat. Acceptable cuts are top round, eye of round, sirloin tip, flank steak and tenderloin. Buy cuts with a minimum of marbling, trimming all visible fat. Choice and prime have generous marbling and are not as healthy as the lesser grades. Marinate less tender cuts of beef in lemon juice, wine vinegar or yogurt to tenderize.*

The sodium content of this recipe will be significantly lower than stated since much of the marinade is discarded. To reduce sodium use low sodium soy sauce.

YIELD: 16 kabobs

Nutritive Values (per kabob)		calories	67.0 kc
total fat	2.5 g	carbohydrates	1.0 g
monosaturated fat	1.0 g	fiber	0.0 g
polyunsaturated fat	0.1 g	protein	9.3 g
saturated fat	0.0 g	sodium	360.2 mg
cholesterol	24.0 mg	sugar	0.3 g

2

SALAD OF COURSE

♥ ANGEL HAIR PASTA AND SEAFOOD

*4 ounces angel hair or cappelini cooked al dente	½ cup sweet red pepper, diced
1 clove garlic, halved	**1½ cups plum tomatoes, peeled, dried and drained
1 sprig basil	⅓ cup sliced black olives
3 tablespoons Italian dressing	½ cup diced cucumber
¾ pound cooked shrimp, crabmeat, mock crabmeat or 1 pound raw, poached and chilled monk fish	1 cup cooked green beans, cut into 1½-inch pieces
	⅓ cup minced parsley
	2 tablespoons pine nuts (garnish)

1. Cook pasta to al dente stage with 1 clove garlic, cut in half, and a sprig of basil in cooking water.

2. In serving dish, combine all ingredients with drained and cooled pasta. Refrigerate for several hours to allow flavors to blend. Garnish with pine nuts.

*SPOTLIGHT (Page 216)

**SPOTLIGHT (Page 203)

SPOTLIGHT *on herbed flavored pasta which you can find on your grocery shelves. Remember that these herbal flavors can cut down on the amount of salt needed to enhance the taste.*

YIELD: 6 servings

Nutritive Values (per serving)		calories	182.0 kc
total fat	6.1 g	carbohydrates	17.0 g
monosaturated fat	1.6 g	fiber	0.6 g
polyunsaturated fat	3.0 g	protein	15.0 g
saturated fat	0.9 g	sodium	191.8 mg
cholesterol	110.7 mg	sugar	0.8 g

SEAFOOD PASTA SALAD

"Riso" (sounds like rizo) or "orzo" is a unique rice shaped macaroni product which is delicious in a hot or cold pasta dish. It may be found in Italian groceries or food specialty stores.

1	cup riso (orzo) pasta
½	pound fresh Italian plum tomatoes, peeled, drained and diced
1	2¼-ounce can pitted black olives, sliced thin
2	tablespoons Italian salad dressing
¼	cup red onion, chopped
⅓	cup red bell pepper, diced
½	cup cucumber, diced
1	pound mock crab, cut in small chunks
¼	cup parsley or cilantro, chopped
¼	teaspoon freshly ground pepper

1. Cook pasta according to package directions. Add a clove of garlic to cooking water for flavor. Discard garlic upon draining. Cool.

2. Mix remaining ingredients.

3. Chill 4 hours or overnight.

Serve on platter or in bowl surrounded by MARINATED VEGETABLES (Pages 78 and 79).

Serve with plates and forks.

SPOTLIGHT *shimmers on an innovative way to flavor pasta while it is cooking. Place a whole peeled and pierced garlic clove into the water along with a few basil leaves or a sprig of thyme or oregano—saves salt and adds flavor to hot or cold pasta.*

YIELD: 6 servings

Nutritive Values (per serving)		calories	273.0 kc
total fat	6.6 g	carbohydrates	40.0 g
monosaturated fat	2.0 g	fiber	1.4 g
polyunsaturated fat	1.6 g	protein	14.9 g
saturated fat	0.6 g	sodium	47.5 mg
cholesterol	15.1 mg	sugar	1.7 g

BIBB LETTUCE AND CRABMEAT SALAD

A specialty of The Well of The Sea in Chicago, this delightful combination can be an hors d'oeuvre or a salad. Serve in living room with a glass of dry white wine.

4   small heads bibb lettuce
*1   6½-ounce can jumbo lump backfin crabmeat
12 cherry tomatoes
2   tablespoons RASPBERRY DIJON VINAIGRETTE
      (Page 235)
1   tablespoon pine nuts

1. Wash, trim and separate lettuce leaves; cut into bite sized pieces. Dry thoroughly. (A lettuce spinner is useful.)

2. Drain crabmeat on paper towels.

3. Place crabmeat, lettuce and cherry tomatoes in salad bowl. When ready to serve, toss with vinaigrette and pine nuts.

*SPOTLIGHT (Page 105)

Though mock crabmeat or monkfish can be substituted, it is sensational made with fresh lump backfin crabmeat.

For a touch of elegance, garnish with a handful of fresh raspberries.

Nutrient values calculated without vinaigrette.

YIELD: 4 servings

Nutritive Values (per serving)		calories	119.0 kc
total fat	5.7 g	carbohydrates	9.7 g
monosaturated fat	1.9 g	fiber	2.2 g
polyunsaturated fat	2.7 g	protein	10.5 g
saturated fat	0.9 g	sodium	244.8 mg
cholesterol	46.1 mg	sugar	3.9 g

MARINATED SCALLOPS AND ARTICHOKE HEARTS

¼ cup vegetable oil
¼ cup olive oil
½ cup red wine vinegar
2 tablespoons Dijon
   mustard
2 tablespoons chopped
   chives
2 tablespoons minced
   onions

½ teaspoon salt
½ teaspoon sugar
   Pepper
2 14-ounce cans
   artichoke hearts
*1½ pound scallops,
   cooked and chilled

1. Combine first 9 ingredients for marinade.

2. Drain artichoke hearts, cut in quarters.

3. Place artichoke hearts, scallops and marinade in a plastic bag. Marinate for several hours or overnight in refrigerator, turning bag occasionally.

4. Drain off excess marinade in colander or cut off corner of plastic bag and drain. Drained marinade may be reserved to store leftovers.

Place in serving bowl. Serve with plates and forks.

*SPOTLIGHT (Page 100)

The fat and sodium content of this recipe will be significantly lower than stated since much of the marinade is discarded. To further reduce sodium content, rinse artichokes.

YIELD: 10 servings

Nutritive Values (per serving)		calories	224.0 kc
total fat	14.2 g	carbohydrates	45.6 g
monosaturated fat	6.7 g	fiber	trace
polyunsaturated fat	4.8 g	protein	18.1 g
saturated fat	1.9 g	sodium	322.0 mg
cholesterol	28.0 mg	sugar	0.3 g

ANTIPASTO BELLA

No matter what you do it turns out great! Serve with party rye or melba toast.

3 carrots, shredded	1 8-ounce can mushrooms
½ cup sweet cocktail onions	1 13-ounce can water packed tuna fish
¼ cup green olives, sliced	¼ cup French dressing, divided
¼ cup pitted ripe olives	2 teaspoons Worcestershire
1 cup celery, sliced	2 tablespoons chili sauce
½ cup sweet pickle relish	2 tablespoons mayonnaise
1½ cups raw cauliflower buds	
½ cup jicama, peeled and cubed	
1 Jerusalem artichoke, peeled and cubed	

1. Marinate carrots for about an hour in enough French dressing to cover.

2. Add remaining ingredients, well drained. (Use mayonnaise, French dressing, Worcestershire and chili sauce to taste to make the mixture moist.)

A can of anchovies, rinsed and well drained, is a tasty addition. Be aware that it will raise the sodium content SPOTLIGHT (Page 140).

Use low sodium canned products and omit olives to reduce sodium content.

YIELD: 12 servings

Nutritive Values (per serving)		calories	146.0 kc
total fat	6.9 g	carbohydrates	13.0 g
monosaturated fat	2.4 g	fiber	1.5 g
polyunsaturated fat	2.5 g	protein	9.6 g
saturated fat	1.2 g	sodium	436.8 mg
cholesterol	14.6 mg	sugar	2.7 g

ANTIPASTO

½ cup chick peas
6 artichoke hearts, halved
1 6-ounce can mushroom caps
4 tablespoons low calorie Italian dressing
1 small head romaine lettuce, shredded
12 cherry tomatoes
12 red onion rings
3 ounces part skim milk mozzarella cheese slices, cut into 1½ inch squares
6 buds pickled cauliflower, halved
12 olives, black and green
1 2-ounce jar sliced pimiento, drained
18 thin slices low fat sausage, rolled into cornucopias

1. Drain chick peas, artichoke hearts and mushrooms; place in plastic bag. Marinate overnight, in 2 tablespoons Italian dressing, turning occasionally to coat.

2. Line a platter with shredded romaine and sprinkle with remaining 2 tablespoons Italian dressing.

3. Drain the marinated vegetables and arrange on romaine with remaining ingredients.

Serve with a loaf of hot garlic bread.

SPOTLIGHT *is brilliant when it serves appetizer and salad as one. Make this "introduction" to your meal a conversation piece and a covert calorie saver by combining two courses.*

To reduce sodium, eliminate olives, use fresh mushrooms, rinse and drain chick peas and artichoke hearts. The fat and sodium content of this recipe will be lower than stated since the marinade is discarded.

YIELD: 8 servings			
Nutritive Values (per serving)		calories	153.0 kc
total fat	6.7 g	carbohydrates	11.5 g
monosaturated fat	2.0 g	fiber	2.8 g
polyunsaturated fat	1.2 g	protein	14.1 g
saturated fat	2.6 g	sodium	620.0 mg
cholesterol	6.6 mg	sugar	2.9 g

TABBOULI

Bulgur is a wheat used in Arab cookery. It is partially cooked, dried and cracked. The most nutritious form has not had the bran removed.

½ cup bulgur (cracked wheat)
1 cup boiling water
½ cup minced scallions
1 cup minced parsley
1 clove minced garlic
½ cup minced fresh mint (optional)
1 cup coarsely chopped peeled tomatoes
¼-⅓ cup fresh lemon juice
½ teaspoon salt
¼ teaspoon freshly ground pepper
¼-½ teaspoon chili powder (optional)
Few drops Tabasco
2 tablespoons olive oil

1. Soak bulgur wheat in water, covered, for 1 hour. Drain and dry in clean dish towel or strainer. Place in bowl and add remaining ingredients except oil. Let stand 30 minutes to allow flavors to blend.

2. Mix in oil.

Serve with PITA TRIANGLES (Page 255).

LENTIL TABBOULI

Substitute ½ cup dried lentils that have been cooked in 1 cup water for 25 to 35 minutes or until tender.

YIELD: 6 servings			
Nutritive Values (per serving)		calories	110.0 kc
total fat	4.9 g	carbohydrates	16.2 g
monosaturated fat	3.3 g	fiber	4.2 g
polyunsaturated fat	0.4 g	protein	2.3 g
saturated fat	0.7 g	sodium	187.3 mg
cholesterol	0.0 mg	sugar	1.9 g

BLACKEYED PEAS VINAIGRETTE

High fiber, high protein and very tasty!

1	16-ounce bag frozen blackeyed peas	1½	cups chopped raw cauliflower
1	clove garlic, split in half	1½	red, green or yellow peppers, cut into julienne strips
1	sprig thyme		Salt or salt substitute, and pepper to taste
1	sprig tarragon		
1	bay leaf	¾	cup corn relish (optional)
3	tablespoons Italian dressing		

1. Cook peas in 1½ cups water with herbs for 30-35 minutes or until tender. (Don't overcook.)

2. Drain and place in plastic bag with Italian dressing, cauliflower, pepper strips and herb seasoning. Marinate in refrigerator several hours or overnight, turning bag occasionally.

Serve as appetizer salad with plates and forks. It is an unusual addition to an antipasto platter.

SPOTLIGHT *is brightly hued on corn relish, a delightful commercial condiment that adds flavor, color and texture to any meal. Watch out, salt sparers.*

The nutrient values include ¼ teaspoon of salt. To reduce sodium use salt substitute.

YIELD: 6 servings

Nutritive Values (per serving)		calories	145.0 kc
total fat	4.2 g	carbohydrates	21.1 g
monosaturated fat	0.9 g	fiber	5.3 g
polyunsaturated fat	2.1 g	protein	7.1 g
saturated fat	0.6 g	sodium	155.3 mg
cholesterol	0.0 mg	sugar	3.6 g

LEMON LENTILS

½ cup lentils
1 cup water
1 clove garlic, cut
   into 2 pieces
2 tablespoons lemon
   juice
Zest of whole lemon
   rind, grated
1 tablespoon olive oil

⅓ cup diced red bell
   pepper
1 tablespoon chopped
   parsley or cilantro
Freshly ground pepper
Salt
* ½ cup corn relish
   (optional)

Cook lentils in water with garlic for 25-35 minutes until just tender. Discard garlic. Drain lentils and place in plastic bag with lemon juice, lemon rind, olive oil and parsley. Season to taste with salt and pepper. Turn bag several times to coat lentils. Chill in refrigerator overnight.

*SPOTLIGHT (Page 48)

LEMON LENTIL DIP

Using steel blade, process all above ingredients in food processor until smooth. Thin with oil to desired consistency. Correct seasonings. A great high fiber dip!

SPOTLIGHT *turns sunshine yellow when it recommends using lemon juice as a salt substitute and flavor enhancer. Fresh lemon peals out with taste. Grate the peel or remove with a zester. Smart cooks freeze squeezed lemon peel because it is easier to grate frozen peel and so convenient to have the extra frozen lemon peel on hand for your next recipe. Rule of thumb; one medium lemon produces about three tablespoons of juice.*

YIELD: 1½ cups

Nutritive Values (per tablespoon)		calories	19.4 kc
total fat	0.6 g	carbohydrates	2.8 g
monosaturated fat	0.4 g	fiber	0.7 g
polyunsaturated fat	0.1 g	protein	1.0 g
saturated fat	0.1 g	sodium	4.0 mg
cholesterol	0.0 mg	sugar	0.3 g

MARINATED MUSHROOMS, ARTICHOKES, AND WATER CHESTNUTS

⅓ cup oil
¼ cup vinegar
½ teaspoon sugar
½ teaspoon salt
1 small onion, thinly sliced
1 teaspoon dill weed

*½ pound small fresh mushrooms, stems removed
1 7-ounce can sliced water chestnuts, drained
1 14-ounce can artichoke hearts, drained and halved

1. Combine first 6 ingredients for marinade.

2. Place vegetables in plastic bag. Pour marinade over vegetables. Put twister on bag; refrigerate several hours or overnight, turning occasionally.

Drain before serving.

May be made 3-4 days in advance.

*SPOTLIGHT (Pages 59, 71)

SPOTLIGHT *on canned vegetables. Keep them conveniently available in your own pantry. However, please be aware that any canned products are high in sodium; rinsing will remove a small amount.*

The fat and sodium content of this recipe will be significantly lower than stated since much of the marinade is discarded.

YIELD: 8 servings			
Nutritive Values (per serving)		calories	100.0 kc
total fat	8.4 g	carbohydrates	5.2 g
monosaturated fat	6.0 g	fiber	0.4 g
polyunsaturated fat	0.7 g	protein	2.5 g
saturated fat	1.2 g	sodium	135.0 mg
cholesterol	0.0 mg	sugar	0.7 g

SALADA de RAPHAEL

*3 large ripe tomatoes, peeled, seeds removed, cut into ½-inch cubes, and drained

1 medium Vidalia or sweet onion, cut into rings

1 each red, yellow and green pepper, cut into ½-inch squares

1 bunch red radishes, sliced

½ jalapeño pepper, seeds removed, diced finely (optional)

¼ teaspoon freshly ground black pepper

½ teaspoon garlic salt

3 tablespoons garlic wine vinegar

1 tablespoon olive oil

½ cup finely chopped cilantro

Place all ingredients in plastic bag; mix well and refrigerate for an hour before serving, turning occasionally.

*SPOTLIGHT (Page 203)

SPOTLIGHT *promises no more tears, just sweetness and delight, with this group of mild onions. Each in its own brief season, Vidalia, Walla Walla, Maui, Spanish or Italian red and Bermuda are gentle varieties that provide sweet flavor for the enhancement of your food.*

YIELD: 6 servings

Nutritive Values (per serving)			
total fat	2.6 g	calories	49.0 kc
monosaturated fat	1.7 g	carbohydrates	6.8 g
polyunsaturated fat	0.4 g	fiber	2.0 g
saturated fat	0.4 g	protein	1.2 g
cholesterol	0.0 mg	sodium	96.0 mg
		sugar	2.8 g

DILLY VEGETABLES

Try some of these newer vegetables. They are fun and taste wonderful! This dish is delicious as either an hors d'oeuvre or as a salad at a buffet supper.

½ cup thinly sliced leeks or sweet onion

1 cup each of any 6 of the following 14 vegetables:

Sliced cucumber
Sliced yellow squash
Sliced celery
Sliced carrots
Sliced mushrooms
Sliced white radishes
Sliced kohlrabi
Sliced Jerusalem artichokes
Sliced jicama
Sliced celeriac
Sliced zucchini
Asparagus tips
Cauliflower buds
Broccoli buds

½ cup Italian dressing (lite dressing optional)

1 cup cherry tomatoes

1 cup drained, sliced black olives

1 13½-ounce can pimiento, cut into 1-inch squares

Dressing:

¼ cup low fat yogurt
⅓ cup mayonnaise
2 tablespoons chili sauce
1 tablespoon fresh lemon juice
½ teaspoon grated lemon rind
1 tablespoon dill weed (3 tablespoons fresh)
½ teaspoon salt
¼ teaspoon freshly ground pepper

1. Place leeks and the 6 cups of vegetables in a plastic bag.

2. Pour the Italian dressing over vegetables. Fasten bag with twister. Refrigerate overnight, turning bag occasionally to coat vegetables with dressing.

DILLY VEGETABLES *(continued)*

*3. A few hours before serving, drain very thoroughly and add the tomatoes, olives and pimientos.

4. Mix dressing ingredients with wire whisk and blend with vegetables.

*A salad spinner is useful for draining vegetables.

SPOTLIGHT *is on high; high fiber, that is. Raw fruits and vegetables provide an excellent source of dietary fiber. Add fiber to your diet and add years to your life.*

The fat and sodium content of this recipe will be significantly lower than stated since much of the marinade is discarded.

YIELD: 20 ½ cup servings

Nutritive Values (per serving)		calories	96.0 kc
total fat	6.1 g	carbohydrates	11.3 g
monosaturated fat	2.3 g	fiber	1.4 g
polyunsaturated fat	1.9 g	protein	2.1 g
saturated fat	0.7 g	sodium	239.0 mg
cholesterol	0.6 mg	sugar	2.1 g

RATATOUILLE SALAD

½	teaspoon thyme	2	red onions, thinly sliced
½	teaspoon rosemary		
1	tablespoon whole cloves	1	teaspoon sugar
1	bay leaf	½	cauliflower, separated into small pieces
½	teaspoon oregano	½	eggplant, peeled and cut into ½ inch cubes
1	cup water		
⅓	cup cider vinegar	1	each red, yellow and green bell pepper, thinly sliced
2¼	cups tomato purée		
½	teaspoon salt	1	13-ounce jar salad olives, sliced
½	teaspoon pepper		

1. To make sauce: put five spices into a cheesecloth bag. Place bag in pot containing next 7 ingredients and bring to a boil. Add vegetables. Simmer 25-30 minutes. Chill.

To your surprise, the vegetables will still be crisp. Can be made ahead. Refrigerated, it lasts for a week.

SPOTLIGHT *suggests making a cheesecloth bag for spices and seasonings in soups from a 6-inch square of cheesecloth. Tie tightly with a string. So easy to remove at the end of cooking time. Gadgets for this purpose are available at gourmet cookware shops.*

The sodium content may be reduced by omitting the olives and using salt substitute.

YIELD: 10 servings

Nutritive Values (per serving)		calories	58.6 kc
total fat	3.2 g	carbohydrates	9.4 g
monosaturated fat	2.0 g	fiber	2.4 g
polyunsaturated fat	0.3 g	protein	2.0 g
saturated fat	0.3 g	sodium	657.0 mg
cholesterol	0.0 mg	sugar	4.4 g

3

FROM THE GOOD EARTH
vegetables and fruits

♥MUSHROOMS au COURANT

Some of our testers think this is one of the best recipes in the book. Try it, you'll like it!

2	tablespoons minced shallots	1/3	cup dry white wine
1	tablespoon olive oil	1	tablespoon fresh lemon juice
1	clove minced garlic	1	teaspoon Dijon mustard
1	tablespoon pine nuts		
* 1½	pounds mushrooms, caps only	2	teaspoons capers (optional)
3	tablespoons currant jelly	1	tablespoon dried currants

1. Using nonstick skillet, sauté shallots in olive oil at moderately high heat for 2 minutes. (If you use an electric skillet, set control at 375°.) Add garlic and pine nuts and continue cooking for 1 minute. **Do not let garlic brown!** Add mushrooms and continue cooking for 5 minutes, turning mushrooms frequently.

2. Add remaining ingredients; continue cooking, basting mushrooms frequently until sauce has a syrupy, glaze-like consistency.

Serve with plates and forks. Can be served with just toothpicks, but you'll miss all that good stuff in the bottom of the dish!

Make ahead and reheat.

* SPOTLIGHT (pages 59, 71)

SPOTLIGHT *gets smart and sweet when currant jelly mixes it up with mushrooms. MUSHROOMS AU COURANT shows our taste buds that opposites are attractive.*

YIELD: 8 servings

Nutritive Values (per serving)		calories	72.2 kc
total fat	2.6 g	carbohydrates	10.5 g
monosaturated fat	1.5 g	fiber	1.2 g
polyunsaturated fat	0.5 g	protein	2.1 g
saturated fat	0.4 g	sodium	61.1 mg
cholesterol	0.0 mg	sugar	4.8 g

♥ MUSHROOMS PROVOLONE

So good they'll lick the pan!

1	pound mushrooms	¾	cup dry white wine
2	tablespoons minced scallions		*Instant blend flour to thicken
1	clove minced garlic	1	cup shredded part skim milk provolone
2	tablespoons margarine		

1. Wash and drain mushrooms. Separate stems and caps (reserve stems for another use).

2. Sauté scallions and garlic in margarine in nonstick electric skillet until limp (set control at 375°). Add wine and simmer five minutes.

3. Add mushroom caps; simmer until mushrooms are tender. Remove mushrooms. Simmer liquid to reduce to ½ cup.

4. Thicken lightly with instant blend flour. Return mushrooms to skillet.

5. Spread provolone cheese over mushrooms. Continue cooking 2-3 minutes or just until cheese is melted.

Prepare through step 4 and finish when ready to serve. Serve with plates and forks.

*SPOTLIGHT (Page 94)

SPOTLIGHT *gives a plug for electric skillets: not only can you cook and serve in the same pan, you can cook right at the table. Also, the non-stick skillet reduces or eliminates fat. Try it — you'll love it!*

Since a portion of the alcohol evaporates in cooking, the calorie and sugar content will be significantly lower than stated.

YIELD: 6 servings

Nutritive Values (per serving)		calories	175.0 kc
total fat	10.2 g	carbohydrates	6.1 g
monosaturated fat	2.8 g	fiber	1.4 g
polyunsaturated fat	2.4 g	protein	11.2 g
saturated fat	4.3 g	sodium	248.7 mg
cholesterol	21.6 mg	sugar	2.0 g

BRANDIED MUSHROOMS

Elegant and easy!

2	tablespoons margarine	⅛	teaspoon tarragon
1	tablespoon oil	2	teaspoons chopped parsley
*1	pound fresh mushrooms, stems removed	4	tablespoons sherry
	Few grinds pepper	1	tablespoon lemon juice
1	tablespoon chopped chives		Few grains sugar
		1	jigger brandy

1. Heat margarine and oil in nonstick skillet. Sauté mushrooms until tender.

2. Add remaining ingredients. Continue to cook 3-4 minutes.

Serve piping hot with toothpicks or plates and forks.

***SPOTLIGHT** on mushrooms. Mushrooms are spongelike in character and very absorbent. In order to prevent excess water being soaked up by mushrooms and diluting your recipes, wash them under running water, a few at a time while rubbing them together between the palms of your hands. Then drain dry before using. Wash only those mushrooms you are going to use. Cover unused mushrooms lightly and refrigerate until ready to use.*

YIELD: 6 servings

Nutritive Values (per serving)		calories	87.0 kc
total fat	6.3 g	carbohydrates	3.9 g
monosaturated fat	3.0 g	fiber	1.0 g
polyunsaturated fat	2.0 g	protein	1.6 g
saturated fat	1.0 g	sodium	53.0 mg
cholesterol	0.0 mg	sugar	1.2 g

PEAS AND MUSHROOM DELIGHTS

Good as an hors d'oeuvre or as a vegetable side dish.

*20 large mushrooms
2 tablespoons margarine
1 clove garlic
1 10-ounce package
    frozen peas
1 teaspoon grated onion
  Nutmeg (freshly
    grated, if possible)

  Salt
  Freshly ground pepper
1 tablespoon sesame
    seed
3 tablespoons freshly
    grated Parmesan

1. Wash and drain mushrooms; remove stems (save for another use).

2. Melt margarine and add garlic that has been cut in half. Allow to stand 30 minutes. Remove garlic.

3. Brush mushroom caps, inside and out, with margarine.

4. Cook peas according to directions on package. Drain.

5. Purée peas and onion in food processor with steel blade. Season with a few grinds of nutmeg, salt and pepper to taste. Add Parmesan and remaining margarine, 1 teaspoon at a time, to produce smooth consistency.

6. Fill mushroom caps with puréed peas. Sprinkle with sesame seed and Parmesan.

7. Place filled mushroom caps in bake and serve dish.

8. Bake at 350° for fifteen minutes.

Prepare in advance through step 7 and refrigerate until cooking time.

*SPOTLIGHT (Pages 59, 71)

YIELD: 20 pieces

Nutritive Values (per piece)		calories	32.0 kc
total fat	1.6 g	carbohydrates	3.2 g
monosaturated fat	0.4 g	fiber	0.9 g
polyunsaturated fat	0.8 g	protein	1.4 g
saturated fat	0.2 g	sodium	48.0 mg
cholesterol	0.2 mg	sugar	1.1 g

MUSHROOMS STUFFED WITH SPINACH

A vegetarian hors d'oeuvre, or an elegant addition to a vegetable platter at dinner.

*1 **pound medium to large (approximately 30) mushroom caps**
½ **measure CREAMED SPINACH (Page 63)**
 Vegetable oil spray
 Freshly grated Parmesan

1. Wash and drain mushrooms. Remove stems and reserve for another use.

2. Spray outside of mushroom caps lightly with vegetable oil. Fill each cap generously with CREAMED SPINACH. Sprinkle lightly with Parmesan.

3. Bake at 375° for 12 to 15 minutes.

Prepare in advance through step 2. Refrigerate covered, then bake when ready to serve.

*SPOTLIGHT (Pages 59, 71)

Nutritive values include creamed spinach. However they will vary according to the capacity of the mushroom cap.

YIELD: 30 mushrooms			
Nutritive Values (per mushroom)		calories	18.0 kc
total fat	0.6 g	carbohydrates	2.4 g
monosaturated fat	0.1 g	fiber	0.7 g
polyunsaturated fat	0.3 g	protein	1.2 g
saturated fat	trace	sodium	61.5 mg
cholesterol	0.2 mg	sugar	0.8 g

♥ EGGPLANT AND SPINACH CRÊPES

2	long eggplants	1½ cups	spaghetti sauce
	Olive oil spray	1 cup	tomato sauce
	Seasoned salt	½ teaspoon	oregano
1	recipe CREAMED	1 teaspoon	basil
	SPINACH (Page 63)	6 ounces	shredded skim milk mozzarella
2	tablespoons freshly grated Parmesan	2 tablespoons	pine nuts

1. Peel eggplants. Slice lengthwise into approximately 20 ¼-inch slices. Spray lightly on both sides with olive oil and sprinkle with seasoned salt. Place on baking sheet; bake in preheated 425° oven for 10 minutes, turning after first 5 minutes. Drain on paper towels to absorb excess oil. Sprinkle lightly with Parmesan.

2. Mix spaghetti sauce, tomato sauce, oregano and basil. Pour ½ cup sauce into ovenproof serving dish.

3. Spoon 2 tablespoons of CREAMED SPINACH in center of each eggplant slice. Roll as a crêpe. Place eggplant crêpes in dish, seam side down. Pour remaining sauce over all. Top with pine nuts.

4. Bake in preheated 375° oven for 20-30 minutes or until heated through. Top with mozzarella during last 3 minutes. **Don't overcook cheese – it will become rubbery!**

Prepare in advance through step 3.

SPOTLIGHT *is on a special way to make crêpes with baked eggplant slices. Sprayed lightly with a small amount of oil and baked briefly, they become flexible and provide a container that can be used like a crêpe. A calorie sparing treat!*

YIELD: 20 crêpes

Nutritive Values (per crêpe)		calories	78.6 kc
total fat	3.4 g	carbohydrates	8.7 g
monosaturated fat	1.3 g	fiber	1.9 g
polyunsaturated fat	0.5 g	protein	4.7 g
saturated fat	1.2 g	sodium	367.0 mg
cholesterol	5.6 mg	sugar	1.8 g

CREAMED SPINACH

This low fat creamed spinach recipe is also a favorite dinner vegetable. (You will want to add a little more milk.)

2   10-ounce packages frozen chopped spinach
1   tablespoon chopped shallots or onions
2   teaspoons margarine
½   teaspoon salt
¼   teaspoon freshly ground pepper
2   tablespoons cornstarch
1¼ cups skim milk

1. Thaw spinach and squeeze out water. Set aside.

2. Sauté chopped shallots or onions in margarine in 2 quart pan (nonstick).

3. Add spinach, salt, pepper and cornstarch; stir until well blended.

4. Stir in milk. Heat to bubbling, stirring frequently to prevent lumping. Reduce heat and simmer for 2 minutes, stirring occasionally.

This recipe can be prepared successfully in microwave oven.

SPOTLIGHT *reduces calories and saturated fat without losing taste when it substitutes skim milk for whole milk or light cream in sauces. For goodness sake, lessen without losing flavor.*

YIELD: 2½ cups

Nutritive Values (per tablespoon)		calories	10.0 kc
total fat	0.2 g	carbohydrates	1.5 g
monosaturated fat	trace	fiber	0.3 g
polyunsaturated fat	0.1 g	protein	0.7 g
saturated fat	trace	sodium	45.0 mg
cholesterol	0.1 mg	sugar	0.3 g

CREAMED SPINACH ON ARTICHOKE BOTTOMS

1	Recipe CREAMED SPINACH (Page 63)		Seasoned bread crumbs
2	6-ounce cans artichoke bottoms		Freshly grated Parmesan
	Olive oil spray		Paprika

1. Drain and rinse artichoke bottoms. Dry on paper towels. Spoon CREAMED SPINACH on each.

2. Place in greased baking dish.

3. Sprinkle with seasoned bread crumbs, Parmesan and paprika.

4. Bake 20 minutes in 350° oven.

Serve with plates and forks.

This also makes a delicious addition to a dinner party's vegetable platter.

SPOTLIGHT on artichoke bottoms: these low fat, low calorie discs are firm delicious containers for many delicacies. Since they are canned in a salt brine, rinse and pat dry before using to reduce sodium.

YIELD: 10 servings

Nutritive Values (per serving)		calories	19.0 kc
total fat	0.4 g	carbohydrates	22.1 g
monosaturated fat	trace	fiber	trace
polyunsaturated fat	0.1 g	protein	1.9 g
saturated fat	trace	sodium	46.0 mg
cholesterol	0.1 mg	sugar	0.3 g

CHEESE STUFFED MUSHROOMS

***24 large mushrooms**
1   recipe MOCK BOURSIN au POIVRE (Page 156)
1   tablespoon margarine
1   tablespoon seasoned bread crumbs

1. Wash mushroom caps and dry. Remove stems.

2. Chop tender portion of mushroom stems and sauté in margarine.

3. Remove from heat and add crumbs and Boursin.

4. Stuff mushroom caps with BOURSIN mixture and place in greased baking dish. Bake for 15 minutes at 350°.

Make ahead and refrigerate until baking time.

Serve with toothpicks or plates and forks.

*SPOTLIGHT (Pages 59, 71)

Nutritive values will vary with size of mushroom cap.

YIELD: 24 mushrooms

Nutritive Values (per mushroom)		calories	25.0 kc
total fat	0.9 g	carbohydrates	2.9 g
monosaturated fat	0.2 g	fiber	0.4 g
polyunsaturated fat	0.3 g	protein	1.6 g
saturated fat	0.3 g	sodium	21.0 mg
cholesterol	1.2 mg	sugar	1.4 g

ARTICHOKES IN GARLIC WINE SAUCE

1	shallot, finely chopped	1	15-ounce can artichokes, quartered
2	large cloves garlic, finely chopped	1	cup shredded part skim milk mozzarella
1	tablespoon margarine	1	tablespoon pine nuts
½	cup dry white wine		

1. Sauté shallot and garlic in margarine in nonstick skillet until wilted. Add wine; bring to boil.

2. Add artichokes, basting to coat with sauce.

3. Simmer for 5 minutes, basting several times.

4. Place in 6-inch bake and serve dish. Heat on top of stove or in 350° oven until piping hot.

5. Top with mozzarella. Heat just until cheese melts (about 2 minutes). Sprinkle with pine nuts.

Prepare in advance through step 3, and reheat when ready to serve.

Serve with plates and forks.

SPOTLIGHT *gives a hint on how to peel garlic cloves easily: place knife handle over garlic clove placed on hard surface; give a light blow with the base of hand to the handle, crushing the clove. Then how easily the "paper" skin may be removed—an "appeeling" suggestion.*

YIELD: 4 servings

Nutritive Values (per serving)		calories	206.3 kc
total fat	14.0 g	carbohydrates	6.3 g
monosaturated fat	4.6 g	fiber	0.0 g
polyunsaturated fat	4.4 g	protein	12.0 g
saturated fat	4.2 g	sodium	190.2 mg
cholesterol	16.2 mg	sugar	0.3 g

ARTICHOKE CANAPE

16 slices party rye bread, toasted on 1 side
1 14-ounce can artichoke hearts, drained
1 egg white
2 tablespoons grated Parmesan
1 tablespoon mayonnaise
1 tablespoon shredded cheddar
Dash cayenne pepper
Paprika

1. Place bread slices on baking sheet toasted side down. Cut artichoke hearts in half; place one half, cut side down, on each slice of bread.

2. Just before serving, beat egg white until stiff. Fold in remaining ingredients except paprika.

3. Top each heart with one half teaspoon of egg white mixture. Sprinkle with paprika.

4. Bake 6-8 minutes until golden brown at 400°.

Bake immediately. A delay will cause egg whites to collapse.

To further reduce fat content use lite mayonnaise and lite cheddar.

YIELD: 16 pieces

Nutritive Values (per piece)		calories	44.0 kc
total fat	1.4 g	carbohydrates	6.5 g
monosaturated fat	0.3 g	fiber	0.5 g
polyunsaturated fat	0.4 g	protein	2.6 g
saturated fat	0.3 g	sodium	113.0 mg
cholesterol	1.6 mg	sugar	0.8 g

POTATO SKINS

A current fad in restaurants. Make them at home!

2 large Idaho baking potatoes	**Coarsely ground pepper**
Vegetable or olive oil spray	**Onion or garlic salt (optional)**

1. Prick potatoes with fork before baking.

2. Bake the potatoes at 400° for 1 hour or until done. Do not grease or wrap in foil. Cut in half.

3. Scoop out almost all of the potato, but leave a little on the peel. (If you leave too much potato they will not be crisp.) Save scooped-out potato pulp for another use.

4. Spray or brush both sides of skins with oil and cut into strips about 3 inches long and 1 inch wide.

5. Sprinkle with the seasoning of your choice.

6. Place on foil lined jelly roll pan and bake at 400° for 10-15 minutes or until crisp.

OPTIONAL TOPPINGS:

Grated Parmesan cheese

Shredded tofu cheddar or part skim milk mozzarella added during the last 2 minutes of baking time

Peanut butter added during last 2 minutes of baking time

CARAWAY DIP (Page 163)

GARLIC SPREAD (Page 172)

SPOTLIGHT *makes you a brilliant chef with multi-purpose potato skins, nature's own container, They are low in fat and contain no cholesterol. High fiber potato skins are filled with nutrients. It's what we put into the potato skin boats that adds fat and cholesterol. Keep it light—keep it right!*

TOFU TIDBITS

Some folks like tofu better than meat!

1 teaspoon cornstarch	1 tablespoon dill weed
½ cup chicken broth	(1 teaspoon dried)
1 clove garlic, chopped	½ teaspoon finely
1 tablespoon chopped	chopped fresh
cilantro or parsley	ginger
1 teaspoon chopped	½ teaspoon cumin
tarragon	*12 ounces extra firm tofu,
(¼ teaspoon dried)	in 1 inch cubes
	Sesame seeds

1. Dissolve cornstarch in 2 tablespoons of chicken broth. Set aside.

2. Combine remaining ingredients, except tofu and sesame seeds, in small saucepan. Bring to boil; add cornstarch mixture gradually, stirring constantly until mixture thickens. Reduce heat and cook for 2 minutes.

3. Remove from heat. Add tofu, spooning sauce gently to coat. Allow to stand for half an hour or longer.

4. Place tofu in single layer on foil lined shallow pan. Sprinkle with sesame seeds. Broil for 5 minutes until lightly browned. Turn tofu over; sprinkle with additional sesame seeds and continue broiling until top surface is browned.

Serve with teriyaki sauce for dipping.

Prepare in advance through step 3.

***SPOTLIGHT:** *Extra firm tofu has had more of the liquid whey extracted.*

YIELD: 8 servings

Nutritive Values (per serving)		calories	67.0 kc
total fat	3.8 g	carbohydrates	2.5 g
monosaturated fat	0.8 g	fiber	0.5 g
polyunsaturated fat	2.0 g	protein	7.0 g
saturated fat	0.5 g	sodium	54.9 mg
cholesterol	trace	sugar	trace

MUSHROOM TRIANGLES

* ½ pound mushrooms,
   finely chopped
¼ cup chopped onion
2 tablespoons
   margarine, divided
1½ tablespoons flour

½ cup skim milk
¼ teaspoon salt
½ teaspoon lemon juice
   Dash pepper
12 very thin slices bread
   Soft margarine

1. Sauté mushrooms and onion in 1 tablespoon margarine. Drain and save juice. Set mushroom mixture aside.

2. Melt remaining margarine, add flour and stir until smooth. Add milk slowly, stir constantly until thickened.

3. Add seasonings, mushrooms and enough of the reserved juice to maintain a pasty consistency.

4. Cut crusts from the bread; spread margarine lightly on one side of each slice.

5. Spread mushroom mixture on unbuttered side of 6 slices; press remaining slices firmly on top, buttered side up.

6. Cut each sandwich into four squares or triangles.

7. Toast on both sides under broiler. Serve hot.

*SPOTLIGHT (Pages 59, 71)

YIELD: 24 sandwiches

Nutritive Values (per piece)		calories	43.7 kc
total fat	2.3 g	carbohydrates	4.9 g
monosaturated fat	0.6 g	fiber	0.3 g
polyunsaturated fat	1.1 g	protein	1.0 g
saturated fat	0.3 g	sodium	93.3 mg
cholesterol	trace	sugar	0.6 g

MUSHROOM SANDWICHES

Yummy!

*1   cup finely chopped mushrooms
1   teaspoon minced onion
2   teaspoons margarine
1   teaspoon minced parsley

Dash Tabasco
**1   tablespoon unflavored low fat yogurt, drained for 5 minutes on paper towels
Party rye bread

1. Sauté mushrooms and onion in margarine in a small nonstick skillet for 5 minutes or until all liquid is absorbed.

2. Add parsley and Tabasco. Stir in yogurt.

3. Spread on rye bread slices. Serve hot or at room temperature.

Garnish with parsley.

*SPOTLIGHT (Page 59)

**ALL ABOUT YOGURT (Page 154)

SPOTLIGHT *puts you in the director's seat with mushrooms, one of the most versatile players in the low fat, low cholesterol, high fiber show. Raw or cooked, hot or cold, they are multi-purpose, a gift of nature.*

YIELD: 15 canapes

Nutritive Values (per piece)			
total fat	0.9 g	calories	32.6 kc
monosaturated fat	0.2 g	carbohydrates	5.1 g
polyunsaturated fat	0.3 g	fiber	0.7 g
saturated fat	trace	protein	1.0 g
cholesterol	trace	sodium	78.0 mg
		sugar	1.2 g

TOASTED MUSHROOM ROLLS

* ½ pound mushrooms, finely chopped
2 tablespoons margarine
3 tablespoons flour
½ teaspoon salt
1 cup skim milk
2 teaspoons minced chives
1 teaspoon lemon juice
1 large loaf sliced fresh whole wheat bread (20 to 24 ounce size)

1. Sauté mushrooms in margarine in nonstick skillet.

2. Blend in flour and salt.

3. Stir in milk. Cook until thick.

4. Add chives and lemon juice. Cool.

5. Remove crusts from slices of bread. Roll thin with rolling pin.

6. Spread with mushroom mixture. Roll up.

7. Pack and freeze if desired.

8. To toast, cut each roll in half and place on greased cookie sheet in 400° oven. Bake 3 to 5 minutes or until lightly browned.

Note: For a more elegant and expensive dish, add ½ pound chopped lobster meat to the mushroom mixture. Follow directions for bread using 2 regular loaves. Proceed as above. Makes about 6 dozen luscious canapés.

*SPOTLIGHT (Pages 59, 71)

To reduce sodium, use salt-free bread and salt substitute.

YIELD: 42 pieces

Nutritive Values (per piece)		calories	39.0 kc
total fat	0.5 g	carbohydrates	7.7 g
monosaturated fat	trace	fiber	1.8 g
polyunsaturated fat	0.1 g	protein	1.8 g
saturated fat	trace	sodium	123.0 mg
cholesterol	0.1 mg	sugar	0.9 g

BEST EVER CUCUMBER PICKLES

These yummy pickles are unforgettable!

¼ cup water	1 teaspoon salt
¾ cup cider vinegar	1 teaspoon cream of tartar
½ cup sugar	
1 teaspoon mustard seed	2 sliced onions
	4 bay leaves
1 teaspoon celery seed	*5 cucumbers

1. Boil all ingredients except cucumbers for 10 minutes; cool to room temperature.

2. Peel cucumbers, halve and remove seeds. Cut into strips of about 1½x2½x¾ inches. Place in plastic bag. Pour cooled marinade over cucumbers. Close bag with twister. Refrigerate for 2 days, turning bag occasionally.

*SPOTLIGHT (Page 243)

ZUCCHINI PICKLES

This same method can be used to make a delicious zucchini pickle.

The nutrient values of sugar and salt will be considerably lower than listed since only a small portion of the marinade will be absorbed.

YIELD: 80 slices

Nutritive Values (per slice)		calories	8.7 kc
total fat	0.1 g	carbohydrates	2.3 g
monosaturated fat	0.0 g	fiber	0.2 g
polyunsaturated fat	0.0 g	protein	0.2 g
saturated fat	0.0 g	sodium	27.5 mg
cholesterol	0.0 mg	sugar	1.6 g

CHERRY TOMATOES BOURSIN

These bite sized tomatoes make a colorful outline for your hors d'oeuvres tray — or they are beautiful (and delicious!) just by themselves.

1   quart large cherry tomatoes
1   recipe MOCK BOURSIN au POIVRE (Page 156)
    *Lemon pepper
¼   cup bread crumbs

1. Cut top third off each cherry tomato; scoop out inside. Sprinkle lightly with lemon pepper. Invert on paper towels and drain for 20 minutes.

2. Fill tomatoes with cheese. Sprinkle lightly with bread crumbs.

3. Bake at 350° for 7 minutes.

*LOW SODIUM LEMON PEPPER (Page 140)

VARIATION:

Fill with CREAMED SPINACH (Page 63). Sprinkle top with freshly grated Parmesan.

YIELD: 25 pieces

Nutritive Values (per piece)		calories	21.0 kc
total fat	0.4 g	carbohydrates	3.2 g
monosaturated fat	trace	fiber	
polyunsaturated fat	trace	protein	1.4 g
saturated fat	0.2 g	sodium	18.0 mg
cholesterol	1.1 mg	sugar	1.8 g

MUSHROOMS IN LEMON MARINADE

Serve mushrooms with toothpicks as an hors d'oeuvre or on a lettuce leaf as a dinner salad.

*1   pound fresh mushrooms
¼   cup olive oil
3   tablespoons lemon juice

1   tablespoon Dijon mustard
½   teaspoon salt
½   teaspoon fresh ground pepper
Dash of Tabasco

1. Wash mushrooms, remove stems, and drain on paper towels (reserve stems for another use). Place caps in plastic bag.

2. Combine remaining ingredients. Pour over mushroom caps in bag. Leave at room temperature 1 hour; refrigerate until ready to use, turning bag occasionally. Drain before serving.

*SPOTLIGHT (Pages 59, 71)

The fat and sodium content of this recipe is significantly lower than stated since much of the marinade is discarded.

YIELD: 6 servings

Nutritive Values (per serving)		calories	103.6 kc
total fat	9.5 g	carbohydrates	4.4 g
monosaturated fat	6.6 g	fiber	1.0 g
polyunsaturated fat	0.9 g	protein	1.8 g
saturated fat	1.3 g	sodium	214.5 mg
cholesterol	0.0 mg	sugar	1.3 g

BRUSSELS SPROUTS PARMESAN

1 20-ounce package frozen Brussels sprouts
3 tablespoons minced pimiento
2 tablespoons minced green pepper
2 tablespoons minced red pepper
2 tablespoons minced green onion
⅓ cup Italian salad dressing
Dash of pepper
3 tablespoons grated Parmesan

1. Cook Brussels sprouts according to directions on package. (Do not overcook).

2. Drain and cool. Place in plastic bag with remaining ingredients. Turn bag to coat with dressing. Refrigerate for 2 days, turning bag occasionally.

3. Drain. Place in serving bowl and top with grated Parmesan.

SPOTLIGHT *on cheese: choose intensely flavored cheeses so that you can use less and still have good flavor. Examples of strongly flavored cheeses are Parmesan, Romano and Sap Sago.*

The sodium and fat content of this recipe will be considerably lower than stated since most of the marinade is discarded. To further reduce sodium, use salt substitute.

YIELD: 8 servings

Nutritive Values (per serving)		calories	89.0 kc
total fat	5.8 g	carbohydrates	7.5 g
monosaturated fat	1.4 g	fiber	2.2 g
polyunsaturated fat	2.9 g	protein	3.6 g
saturated fat	1.2 g	sodium	137.5 mg
cholesterol	1.9 mg	sugar	1.7 g

BRUSSELS SPROUTS PARISIENNE

1   pound fresh Brussels sprouts
1   recipe MOCK BOURSIN AU POIVRE (Page 156)
    Lemon Pepper

1. Cook Brussels sprouts in boiling salted water for three minutes. Drain; chill in ice water. Drain in colander and invert on paper towels.

2. Hollow out center of each sprout and trim core so that it will stand upright.

3. Stuff center of each sprout with 1 teaspoon cheese mixture. Sprinkle lightly with lemon pepper.

Refrigerate covered until ready to use. Allow to stand at room temperature for half an hour before serving.

SPOTLIGHT *"blanches" but retains color and crispness when it advises immersing vegetables briefly (1-3 minutes) in boiling water. Drain. Cool vegetables in water with ice cubes immediately. The cook stays out of hot water and receives applause!*

YIELD: 30 pieces

Nutritive Values (per piece)		calories	16.0 kc
total fat	0.3 g	carbohydrates	2.5 g
monosaturated fat	trace	fiber	0.8 g
polyunsaturated fat	trace	protein	1.2 g
saturated fat	trace	sodium	14.0 mg
cholesterol	0.9 mg	sugar	2.0 g

MARINATED VEGGIES

This method of marinating vegetables preserves their color and crispness. Try it. It's wonderful!

1½ cups each:
   Pea pods, strings removed
   Broccoli buds
   Cauliflower buds
   Carrot rings
   White radish slices
   Cucumber, peeled, quartered, seeded and sliced

1 tablespoon salt
1 cup cider vinegar
½ cup sugar
½ cup water

1. Combine vegetables and salt in plastic bag. Turn several times to distribute salt. Let stand at room temperature for 6 hours, turning bag occasionally.

2. Drain; rinse with water several times to remove salt; drain well. Place in clean plastic bag.

3. Mix sugar, water and vinegar. Pour over vegetables. Tie twister on bag. Refrigerate overnight. Drain before serving.

Reserve liquid to store leftover vegetables.

The sodium and sugar content of this recipe will be lower than stated since much of the marinade is discarded.

YIELD: 12 ¾ cup servings

Nutritive Values (per serving)		calories	52.8 kc
total fat	0.2 g	carbohydrates	14.0 g
monosaturated fat	trace	fiber	1.9 g
polyunsaturated fat	trace	protein	1.4 g
saturated fat	trace	sodium	546.0 mg
cholesterol	0.0 mg	sugar	9.6 g

VEGETABLES TO MARINATE

Yes, there are certain vegetables whose flavors and textures "bloom" well when marinated. Remember that most of the oil and sodium from the marinade is not absorbed by the finished product.

SUGGESTED VEGETABLES:

Artichoke Hearts

Asparagus spears

Broccoli buds

Cauliflower buds

Carrot slices

Cooked beans or legumes with minced onion

Cucumber slices

Green beans, fresh or canned Blue Lake

Jerusalem artichoke slices

Jicama slices

Mushroom caps

Onion slices (red or Vidalia)

Pimiento squares

Red, yellow or green pepper squares or slices

White radish slices

SUGGESTED MARINADES:

RASPBERRY VINAIGARETTE (Page 235)

LEMON MARINADE (Page 75)

Green goddess dressing

Italian dressing

Vinaigrette

PREPARATION:

Place prepared vegetables in a plastic bag with ¼-½ cup of dressing or marinade of your choice. Close bag with a twister and turn over several times to coat vetgetables. Refrigerate overnight, turning ocasionally. Drain before using.

VEGGIE MEDLEY

Your vegetarian friends will "eat up" this make-ahead variety platter of low fat treats. Great for a tail-gater.

STUFFED CELERY

1. Cut off root end. Separate into stalks.

2. Wash and dry on paper towels. Remove coarse strings with vegetable peeler.

3. Fill with desired stuffing (see below).

4. Cut into 1 to 3 inch lengths.

5. Garnish with paprika or sesame seeds if desired.

STUFFED ENDIVE

1. Cut off root end. Separate leaves.

2. Wash and drain dry on paper towels.

3. Fill with desired stuffings (see below).

STUFFED MUSHROOM CAPS

*1. Wash mushrooms. Remove stems. Invert on paper towel to dry.

2. Fill with desired stuffing (see below).

*SPOTLIGHT (Page 59)

SUGGESTED STUFFINGS:

MOCK BOURSIN (Page 156)

WATERCRESS ROLLUPS, step 1 (Page 171)

SEAFOOD ALMOND BOAT filling, step 1 (Page 116)

HUMMUS BI TAHINI (Page 149)

VEGGIE MEDLEY (continued)

CHERRY TOMS

This is a low calorie appetizer, about 16 calories per piece.
Can be prepared ahead. Serve on lettuce and chopped ice.

1	pint cherry tomatoes	2	tablespoons chopped green onion
¼	cup lite mayonnaise		
1	teaspoon lemon juice	*1	7½-ounce can crabmeat, drained
¼	teaspoon salt		
	A few drops Tabasco		

1. Slice off tops of tomatoes gently. Remove insides with a small spoon or grapefruit knife. Salt lightly and let drain upside down on paper towels.

2. Blend remaining ingredients.

3. Stuff tomatoes with crab mixture.

4. Refrigerate.

*SPOTLIGHT (Page 105)

TUNA TOMATO TREATS

2	pints cherry tomatoes	2	teaspoons Dijon mustard
	Salt		
2	7-ounce cans water packed tuna, drained and flaked	1½	tablespoons chopped capers
			Olive slices
¼	cup lite mayonnaise		Red or green pepper

1. Slice off tops of tomatoes gently. Remove insides with a small spoon or grapefruit knife. Salt lightly and let drain upside down on paper towels.

2. In bowl, mix tuna, mayonnaise, mustard and capers.

3. Stuff tomatoes with mixture and garnish some with an olive slice and others with capers or strip of red or green pepper.

4. Refrigerate until ready to serve.

Nutritive content for celery, endive, mushrooms, radishes and cherry tomatoes is minimal. Nutritive value for total recipe is dependent upon stuffings used.

STUFFED RED RADISHES

Radishes
MOCK BOURSIN (Page 156)

1. Carefully scoop out radishes with vegetable peeler, leaving firm shell.

2. Stuff with softened cheese spread.

TUNA ZUCCHINI SLICES

2-3 small straight zucchinis
1   7-ounce can water packed tuna, drained
3   tablespoons low fat yogurt drained 5 minutes on paper towels
Salt free herb seasoning to taste

1. Cut zucchini in half lengthwise. Scoop out seeds.

2. Blend remaining ingredients in a food processor.

3. Fill zucchini with tuna. Cover and chill 1½ hours. Slice in 1 inch pieces.

DILLY CUCUMBER SPEARS

1   long cucumber
Seasoned salt
Dill weed

1. Peel cucumber. Cut in half, or thirds (depending on length) crosswise. Cut lengthwise in finger-size pieces.

2. Sprinkle with seasoned salt and dill weed.

3. Serve immediately to avoid weeping.

CURRIED BABY BEETS

2 16-ounce cans red
     beets, drained
   Herb-tinctured
     vinegar
*1 cup low fat yogurt,
     drained 2 hours

Curry powder to taste
Horseradish
Salt
Pepper

1. Drain beets and marinate in herb-tinctured vinegar.

2. Before serving, drain and put toothpick into each beet. Arrange around bowl of low fat yogurt seasoned with curry powder, a dash of grated horseradish, salt and pepper.

Be sure to rinse beets several times so that beet juice doesn't discolor the dip! This same marinade may be used with canned Blue Lake string beans. Remember to rinse off excess salt.

*ALL ABOUT YOGURT (Page 154)

To reduce sodium, substitute low sodium canned beets or boiled fresh beets.

YIELD: 40 pieces

Nutritive Values (per piece)		calories	10.6 kc
total fat	0.1 g	carbohydrates	2.2 g
monosaturated fat	trace	fiber	0.2 g
polyunsaturated fat	trace	protein	0.5 g
saturated fat	0.1 g	sodium	79.7 mg
cholesterol	0.4 mg	sugar	1.8 g

FRESH FRUIT APPETIZER

An appetizer fruit salad is the perfect starter for a hot weather dinner. Arrange an assortment of the following fruits, cut up or whole, to your own taste and design:

Apples	*Nectarines*
Apricots	*Grapes (red blaze especially)*
Blueberries	*Kiwi slices*
Strawberries	*Pineapple chunks*
Raspberries (sprinkle on top as they are most perishable)	*Orange sections*
	Grapefruit sections, pink or white
Melon balls, slices or chunks	*Plum wedges*
Peach chunks or wedges	

May be served in a bowl, as an individual fruit plate, or as chunks on individual kabob sticks.

Serve with FRUITED YOGURT SAUCE (Page 244).

SPOTLIGHT *on fresh fruit preparation: to prepare apples, peaches and nectarines in advance, peel and slice, then sprinkle with enough lemon juice or diluted raspberry vinegar to coat. This acid bath retards the discoloration process caused by oxidation.*

PINEAPPLE WITH CHUTNEY DIP

*3   cups low fat yogurt,
     drained for 4 hours
¼   cup chutney or
     MANGO CHUTNEY
     (Page 237)

¼   teaspoon dry mustard
1   teaspoon curry powder
¼   cup toasted almonds,
     coarsely chopped
1   ripe pineapple

1. To make CHUTNEY DIP, blend first 5 ingredients well.

2. Chill for 4 hours.

3. Cut pineapple in half. Scoop out meat. Cut into chunks.

4. Fill half pineapple shell with dip.

5. Place on platter and surround with toothpicked pineapple chunks.

*ALL ABOUT YOGURT (Page 154)

YIELD: 8 servings

Nutritive Values (per serving)		calories	108.0 kc
total fat	3.5 g	carbohydrates	15.0 g
monosaturated fat	1.6 g	fiber	1.2 g
polyunsaturated fat	1.2 g	protein	5.5 g
saturated fat	1.1 g	sodium	65.0 mg
cholesterol	5.3 mg	sugar	10.8 g

BABY ARTICHOKES

While the season for baby artichokes is brief (March, April, May), they are worth the wait. Unlike mature artichokes, they are completely edible. Select the firm and heavy babies. They can vary from walnut to jumbo egg size.

TO COOK BABY ARTICHOKES:

1. Rinse in cold water.

2. Remove outer green leaves down to a point where leaves are half green at the top and half yellow.

3. Cut off green, fibrous, top pointed cone of leaves.

4. Cut off stem even with the artichoke bottom.

5. Remove any tough pink or purple leaves.

6. Place in pot with water to cover. Add juice of 1 lemon and 1 halved garlic clove.

7. Boil gently 10-15 minutes. Test for doneness with toothpick at stem end.

8. Drain.

Serve quartered, halved or whole, depending upon size, with toothpicks or with plates and forks. We suggest dipping in HORSERADISH HOLLANDAISE (Page 238) for hot artichokes or ARTICHOKE SMOOTHY (Page 165) for cold.

MARINATED BABY ARTICHOKES

1. Drain cooked artichokes. Halve or quarter according to desired size.

2. Place in plastic bag with Italian salad dressing to coat. Put twister on bag. Marinate in refrigerator overnight, turning occasionally. This will keep, refrigerated, for several weeks if you continue to turn occasionally.

4

LOOK TO THE SEA
fish and seafood

♡ MUSSELS IN GARLIC WINE SAUCE

Cook and serve in your electric skillet.

Finger lickin' delicious! Have wet towels available for clean up unless they lick their fingers clean.

2-3 cloves garlic, finely chopped	**Few grinds pepper**
¼ cup chopped scallions, white part only or Vidalia onion	**1 cup dry white wine**
1 tablespoon margarine	**2 pounds mussels in shells, cleaned**
	***Instant blend flour to thicken (optional)**

1. In nonstick skillet, sauté garlic and scallions in margarine for 2 minutes. Add pepper and wine; boil to reduce one half.

2. Add cleaned mussels to skillet. Bring to boil and cook, covered, for 3 minutes until shells open. Discard any unopened shells.

3. Push mussels to the side of the pan, and thicken pan juices with instant blend flour.

May be done in advance through step 2. Serve with French bread to soak up juices.

*SPOTLIGHT (Page 94)

VARIATION: CLAMS IN GARLIC WINE SAUCE

Substitute 2 pounds clams for mussels.

> **SPOTLIGHT** *on cleaning mussels. Rinse off sand. Remove beards when necessary. Throw out any mussels with broken shells. After cooking, discard mussels with unopened shells.*

YIELD: 6 servings

Nutritive Values (per serving)		calories	179.0 kc
total fat	5.3 g	carbohydrates	7.1 g
monosaturated fat	1.3 g	fiber	0.2 g
polyunsaturated fat	2.0 g	protein	18.3 g
saturated fat	0.8 g	sodium	482.0 mg
cholesterol	42.0 mg	sugar	0.5 g

TANGY TUNA PUFF

1   6½-ounce can water packed tuna, drained
*1   cup low fat yogurt, drained 24 hours
2   tablespoons lite mayonnaise
3   tablespoons prepared horseradish

1. Blend all ingredients in food processor using steel blade.

2. Place in 2 cup soufflé dish that has been sprayed with vegetable oil.

3. Bake at 300° for 30 minutes.

Serve with party rye.

Prepare in advance through step 2 and bake when ready to serve.

*ALL ABOUT YOGURT (Page 154)

SPOTLIGHT *flashes the news to choose water packed canned tuna in order to cut down on oil. For sodium conscious dieters, purchase low sodium canned tuna.*

Use low sodium, water packed tuna to reduce sodium.

YIELD: 1½ cups			
Nutritive Values (per tablespoon)		calories	20.0 kc
total fat	0.5 g	carbohydrates	0.9 g
monosaturated fat	trace	fiber	0.0 g
polyunsaturated fat	trace	protein	2.8 g
saturated fat	0.1 g	sodium	54.6 mg
cholesterol	1.0 mg	sugar	0.5 g

SCALLOP KABOBS

Serve on miniature skewers for "guest do-it-yourself" appetizers. If made on large skewers, they can be served as an entrée with rice.

2 pounds sea scallops	24 cherry tomatoes
24 large stuffed green olives	12 lemon wedges

SOY BASTING SAUCE

¼ cup soy sauce	¼ cup minced parsley
¼ cup oil	Dash of pepper
¼ cup lemon juice	

1. Combine SOY BASTING SAUCE ingredients in plastic bag or bowl. Add scallops and marinate for one hour, turning frequently.

2. Alternate scallops, olives and tomatoes on oiled skewers.

3. Brush generously with SOY BASTING SAUCE before broiling and frequently while cooking to keep scallops moist. Oven broil or grill 2 to 4 inches from heat 2 to 3 minutes on each side, just long enough to brown scallops, as overcooking toughens them.

Serve with lemon wedges.

To reduce sodium use low sodium soy sauce. Note that only a portion of the evaluated sodium in this recipe is absorbed by the finished product.

YIELD: 12 8-inch kabobs

Nutritive Values (per kabob)		calories	146.0 kc
total fat	8.2 g	carbohydrates	6.4 g
monosaturated fat	3.2 g	fiber	1.3 g
polyunsaturated fat	3.1 g	protein	14.4 g
saturated fat	1.0 g	sodium	949.0 mg
cholesterol	24.5 mg	sugar	1.4 g

SCALLOPS POLONAISE

A delightful hors d'oeuvre or a main course for a buffet supper. You'll never make too much!

1 teaspoon margarine	**Instant blend flour to thicken
*1 pound sliced mushrooms	1 tablespoon chopped fresh parsley (1 teaspoon dried)
½ cup chopped shallots	
1 green pepper, cut in julienne strips	1 small jar sliced pimiento, drained
½ cup dry white wine	
3 tablespoons lemon juice	2 tablespoons powdered buttermilk
1½ teaspoons fresh tarragon (½ teaspoon dried)	1 teaspoon caraway seed
	¼ teaspoon freshly ground pepper
½ teaspoon onion salt	Salt to taste
2 pounds fresh sea scallops	

1. Sauté mushrooms, shallots and green peppers in margarine in nonstick skillet.

2. Place next 4 ingredients in 2 quart saucepan. Add liquid from sautéed mushroom mixture. Heat to boiling. Add ½ pound of scallops; return to boil. Reduce heat and simmer, covered, for 2 minutes; remove from heat. Leave in broth for 5 minutes. Remove scallops with slotted spoon and continue poaching remaining scallops in ½ pound batches. Cut scallops into bite-sized pieces.

3. Drain liquid from poached scallops back into pot; bring to boil over medium heat. Thicken lightly with instant blend flour. Cool a little and add powdered buttermilk, stirring to prevent lumps.

SCALLOPS POLONAISE *(continued)*

4. Add poached scallops, parsley, pimiento, caraway seed, pepper and sautéed vegetables to thickened sauce. Stir gently to coat. Heat just to simmer (do not boil after adding buttermilk powder—it will curdle).

Place in heated serving dish and keep hot on electric hot tray.

Can be served with plates and forks or used as a filling in CROUSTADES (Page 252)

*SPOTLIGHT (Page 59, 71)

**SPOTLIGHT (Page 94)

SPOTLIGHT *on cultured buttermilk powder: did you ever wonder why grandma's baked goods had such a fine uniform texture? It was the real buttermilk, a by-product of butter churning. There is now available a powdered product, the by-product of Wisconsin buttermaking. Low in fat and cholesterol, store it in your refrigerator and you'll always have the real thing on hand. We use it in our TURKEY STROGANOFF (Page 28) recipe for the tart flavor and white color of sour cream. Fool the eye and the palate!*

YIELD: 8 servings

Nutritive Values (per serving)		calories	159.0 kc
total fat	2.8 g	carbohydrates	9.6 g
monosaturated fat	0.5 g	fiber	1.3 g
polyunsaturated fat	1.2 g	protein	22.0 g
saturated fat	0.4 g	sodium	259.0 mg
cholesterol	39.0 mg	sugar	1.8 g

SCALLOPS IN MUSHROOM CAPS

It makes a delicious main course as well

24 mushroom caps, silver dollar size
2 tablespoons Italian salad dressing
24 sea scallops to fit mushroom caps
Seasoned bread crumbs

Vegetable oil spray
Seasoned salt
Sesame seeds
1 tablespoon Parmesan
Instant blend flour to thicken

1. Place mushrooms in plastic bag with Italian dressing. Tip bag to coat mushrooms. Marinate for 1-2 hours, turning several times to distribute dressing.

2. Place mushroom caps in oven proof serving dish. Cover loosely with foil. Bake in preheated 450° oven for 5 minutes. Pour off juice from mushrooms.

3. Roll scallops in bread crumbs. Place a scallop in each mushroom cap. Spray with oil; sprinkle lightly with seasoned salt; sprinkle with sesame seed and Parmesan.

4. Bake at 450°, uncovered, for 4 minutes. Thicken pan juices with instant blend flour. Baste mushrooms with thickened juice.

SPOTLIGHT *on instant blend flour. You'll never make a white sauce again! This is a highly pulverized form of flour that permits quick, lump-free thickening of sauces, soups and gravies. Wondra™ is an example of instant blend flour.*

Nutritive analysis based on 12 scallops per pound.

YIELD: 24 pieces			
Nutritive Values (per piece)		calories	57.0 kc
total fat	1.4 g	carbohydrates	3.5 g
monosaturated fat	0.4 g	fiber	0.7 g
polyunsaturated fat	0.5 g	protein	7.5 g
saturated fat	0.2 g	sodium	166.0 mg
cholesterol	12.7 mg	sugar	0.6 g

SEAFOOD-STUFFED MUSHROOMS

1	cup coarsely chopped cooked scallops or mock crab	1	teaspoon lemon juice
1	tablespoon cracker crumbs	1	teaspoon minced tarragon
1	tablespoon minced fresh onion		Salt to taste
1	tablespoon finely chopped parsley	1	egg white
1	tablespoon soft margarine	*20	large mushroom caps, stems removed
			Buttered crumbs or **toasted sesame seeds (optional)

1. Mix the first nine ingredients together.

2. Fill mushroom caps with the mixture; sprinkle with buttered crumbs (mix ¼ cup bread crumbs with 1 tablespoon melted margarine) or sesame seeds.

3. Bake in 350° oven 15-20 minutes.

Prepare in advance through step 2. Refrigerate.

*SPOTLIGHT (Pages 59, 71)

**SPOTLIGHT (Page 151)

SPOTLIGHT on "mock crab" and "mock lobster," attractive substitutes for the much higher priced shell fish: low in fat and cholesterol, high in protein, these crab and lobster delights are fully cooked and ready to eat, hot or cold. Beware, sodium watchers, these seafood products are higher in sodium than the real thing.

YIELD: 20 mushrooms

Nutritive Values (per mushroom)		calories	29.0 kc
total fat	0.9 g	carbohydrates	2.1 g
monosaturated fat	0.2 g	fiber	0.5 g
polyunsaturated fat	0.3 g	protein	3.5 g
saturated fat	0.1 g	sodium	68.0 mg
cholesterol	6.0 mg	sugar	0.5 g

BITES O' CRAB

*8 ounces crabmeat, fresh, frozen, canned or mock crab

2 English muffins, sliced horizontally into 3 thin rounds

½ cup (2 ounces) part skim mozzarella or low fat colby cheese, shredded

2 tablespoons lite mayonnaise

1½ teaspoons chopped chives

2 drops Tabasco
Dash pepper

¼ teaspoon salt

2 egg whites

1. Drain and chop crabmeat coarsely.

2. Place sliced muffins on a baking sheet. Bake at 400° for 6-9 minutes or until lightly browned.

3. Combine cheese, mayonnaise, chives, Tabasco, pepper and crabmeat. Mix thoroughly.

4. Add salt to egg whites and beat until stiff but not dry.

5. Fold crab mixture into egg whites.

6. Spread each muffin with crab mixture.

7. Bake at 450° for 8-10 minutes or until lightly browned. Cut into quarters before serving.

Bake promptly after beaten egg whites are added.

Prepare through step 3 and complete when ready to serve.

*SPOTLIGHT (Pages 95, 105)

*COMPARISON CHART (Page 139)

Nutritive analysis calculated with mock crabmeat. For lower sodium content use canned or fresh crabmeat.

YIELD: 24 canapés			
Nutritive Values (per canapé)		calories	25.0 kc
total fat	1.0 g	carbohydrates	2.5 g
monosaturated fat	0.2 g	fiber	trace
polyunsaturated fat	0.3 g	protein	1.3 g
saturated fat	0.3 g	sodium	71.9 mg
cholesterol	1.4 mg	sugar	0.2 g

DEVILED CRAB

When you go to the seashore, collect some scallop shells. They become the perfect "dish" for this deviled crab mixture—a sure winner!

⅓ cup each diced green and red pepper
1 tablespoon chopped shallots
3 tablespoons margarine, divided
¾ cup bread crumbs, divided
½ cup skim milk
2 tablespoons minced parsley

¼ teaspoon salt
⅛ teaspoon freshly ground pepper
1½ tablespoons Worcestershire
1 teaspoon Dijon mustard
2 cups (1 pound) crabmeat or mock crab, coarsely chopped

1. Sauté red and green peppers and shallots in 1 tablespoon margarine until softened. Set aside.

2. Sauté bread crumbs in remaining margarine until lightly browned. Reserve ¼ cup for topping.

3. Combine next 6 ingredients with sautéed vegetables and bread crumbs. Stir in chopped crab.

4. Spoon into individual sea shells. Top with remaining bread crumbs. Sprinkle with paprika.

5. Bake in preheated 350° oven for 15 minutes or until heated.

This crab stuffing can also be used as a stuffing for mushroom caps or cooked pasta shells.

May be prepared in advance through step 4.

Computed with mock crab. See COMPARISON CHART (Page 139).

YIELD: 8 servings			
Nutritive Values (per serving)		calories	118.5 kc
total fat	5.3 g	carbohydrates	9.8 g
monosaturated fat	1.2 g	fiber	0.4 g
polyunsaturated fat	2.4 g	protein	7.9 g
saturated fat	0.5 g	sodium	667.0 mg
cholesterol	11.6 mg	sugar	1.1 g

CRAB CANAPES

½ teaspoon minced onion	* ½ cup flaked crabmeat or mock crab, chopped
1 tablespoon margarine	4 thin slices toasted bread, crusts removed
1½ teaspoons flour	2 tablespoons grated Parmesan
½ teaspoon curry powder	
⅛ teaspoon salt	
¼ cup skim milk	

1. Sauté onion in margarine until cooked.

2. Combine flour, curry powder and salt and stir into onion; cook until bubbly.

3. Slowly pour in milk, stirring constantly. Mix in crabmeat.

4. Cut toast slices into quarters. Spread crab mixture on toast squares and sprinkle with Parmesan.

5. Place on cookie sheet and broil 2-3 minutes. Serve hot.

*SPOTLIGHT (Pages 95, 105)

Nutritive values calculated using canned crab.

YIELD: 16 canapes			
Nutritive Values (per canape)		calories	33.0 kc
total fat	1.3 g	carbohydrates	3.6 g
monosaturated fat	0.3 g	fiber	0.2 g
polyunsaturated fat	0.5 g	protein	1.8 g
saturated fat	0.3 g	sodium	99.0 mg
cholesterol	4.9 mg	sugar	0.4 g

TOASTIE TUNAS

3   dozen bread rounds, 1½ inches

1   6½-ounce can water packed tuna, drained

2   tablespoons onion, finely chopped

2   tablespoons green pepper, chopped

1   tablespoon pimiento, chopped

¼   cup lite mayonnaise

*¼   cup low fat yogurt, drained 5 minutes on paper towel

1   teaspoon Worcestershire

2   teaspoons lemon juice
Dash of pepper

¼   cup grated part skim milk mozzarella

2   egg whites, stiffly beaten
Parmesan cheese (optional)

1. Place bread rounds on a cookie sheet and broil until lightly browned on one side.

2. Combine next 9 ingredients. Blend well.

3. Fold in stiffly beaten egg whites.

4. Top untoasted side of bread rounds with a mound of the mixture. Sprinkle with Parmesan cheese.

5. Broil about 4 inches from heat until puffed and browned.

Prepare in advance through step 2. Just before serving, continue at step 3.

Variation: Substitute crab meat, mock crab, salmon,or any other cooked fish. A tasty use for left over fish!

*ALL ABOUT YOGURT (Page 154)

YIELD: 36 canapes

Nutritive Values (per piece)		calories	44.0 kc
total fat	1.4 g	carbohydrates	5.2 g
monosaturated fat	0.2 g	fiber	0.3 g
polyunsaturated fat	0.5 g	protein	2.6 g
saturated fat	0.3 g	sodium	81.0 mg
cholesterol	2.7 mg	sugar	0.5 g

SEAFOOD CATALINA

Serve with plates and forks to the luckiest guests on your list. They will love it!

1	14-ounce can artichoke hearts, quartered		*1	pound poached sea scallops, cut into bite size pieces
1	8-ounce can mushroom caps		1	pound crab or mock crab
1	14-ounce can hearts of palm, sliced in ½ inch pieces.		12	large cooked shrimp, halved
				Seasoned salt to taste
¾	cup chopped Vidalia or sweet onion		½	cup low calorie Catalina dressing to moisten
				Chopped parsley

1. Drain vegetables and dry on paper towels.

2. Place all ingredients, except parsley, in plastic bag and allow to marinate overnight, turning occasionally to coat with dressing. Serve, garnished with parsley.

> ***SPOTLIGHT** *on poaching scallops: place ½ cup dry white wine in saucepan. Tie in cheesecloth bag: 1 sprig fresh tarragon (1 teaspoon dried), 1 slice onion, 1 wedge lemon, a sprig of celery leaves and 1 bay leaf. Heat to boiling. Add scallops, ½ pound at a time. Return to boil, then reduce heat and simmer, covered, for 5 minutes. Remove from heat. Leave in broth for 5 minutes. Remove scallops with slotted spoon. Repeat above for remaining scallops.*

YIELD: 12 servings

Nutritive Values (per serving)		calories	95.2 kc
total fat	1.5 g	carbohydrates	6.0 g
monosaturated fat	0.2 g	fiber	0.6 g
polyunsaturated fat	0.4 g	protein	14.5 g
saturated fat	0.1 g	sodium	261.8 mg
cholesterol	48.4 mg	sugar	2.7 g

TEA POACHED SALMON

1	tablespoon tea leaves	3	slices fresh ginger root
2	tablespoons honey	2	pounds salmon fillets
1	cinnamon stick (broken in half)		

1. Mix first 4 ingredients (marinade); pour into large plastic bag. Place salmon in bag, seal with twister and turn bag several times to coat salmon well. Refrigerate for 1 hour, turning occasionally.

2. Place a rack in a heavy skillet with a rock or some crumpled foil underneath to elevate it 1½ inches.

3. Add 1 inch of water and marinade to skillet; bring to boil.

4. Place salmon on rack, skinside down. Cover skillet and steam 10-12 minutes or until fish flakes.

Serve at room temperature with CUCUMBER DILL SAUCE (Page 243).

SPOTLIGHT on poaching seafood: cooking time must be brief. Simmer, don't boil for finest texture and flavor. Then you won't have to fish for great results!

The fat, sugar and sodium content of this recipe will be significantly lower than stated since much of the marinade is discarded.

YIELD: 12 servings

Nutritive Values (per serving)		calories	115.0 kc
total fat	3.7 g	carbohydrates	4.7 g
monosaturated fat	1.6 g	fiber	0.0 g
polyunsaturated fat	0.9 g	protein	14.2 g
saturated fat	0.8 g	sodium	128.5 mg
cholesterol	39.8 mg	sugar	3.2 g

WHOLE SALMON POACHED IN COOKING BAG

1	3-pound salmon	2	tablespoons lemon juice
	Salt and pepper	½	lemon rind
1	sprig each dill, parsley and thyme	½	cup dry white wine
1	stalk celery with leaves	1-2	tablespoons chutney or MANGO CHUTNEY (Page 237)
1	small slice onion		
1	tablespoon flour		

1. Wash salmon and drain dry. Sprinkle inside with salt and pepper. Place herbs, celery, onion and lemon rind in fish.

2. Shake 1 tablespoon flour in large size Reynolds Oven Cooking Bag and place in two-inch deep roasting pan.

3. Place salmon in bag and pour lemon juice and wine into bag. Close bag with twister and cut six half-inch slits in top of bag.

*4. Bake 35 to 40 minutes in preheated 350° oven or until fish tests done. Cut corner of bag and pour broth into cup; strain; chill to thicken slightly.

5. Place fish on serving platter. Discard herbs and vegetables from inside of fish. Remove skin and allow fish to cool.

6. Spread a thin layer of jellied broth on surface of fish. Refrigerate until set.

WHOLE SALMON *(continued)*

7. Mix remaining broth with 1-2 tablespoons chutney.
   Spread this second layer of glaze over surface of fish.
   Chill to set. Refrigerate, covered, until ready to serve.

Serve with an assortment of sauces:

CUCUMBER DILL SAUCE (Page 243)

MANGO CHUTNEY (Page 237)

PLUM TOMATO SALSA (Page 240)

*To determine baking time for whole fish, measure thickest
part. Bake 13 minutes per inch. Test for doneness by cutting
along bone into thickest part of fish. It should flake and
appear dull in color.

> **SPOTLIGHT** *carries a torch for
> cooking bags; they are easy to use, make
> clean-up a breeze (no pots and pans to
> wash), make marinating and cooking in
> the same bag a snap. The product is a
> moist, tender delight. For the busy,
> discriminating cook, cooking bags are a
> must!*

YIELD: 12 servings

Nutritive Values (per serving)		calories	147.6 kc
total fat	5.0 g	carbohydrates	0.5 g
monosaturated fat	2.4 g	fiber	trace
polyunsaturated fat	1.4 g	protein	20.1 g
saturated fat	1.2 g	sodium	63.7 mg
cholesterol	59.7 mg	sugar	0.2 g

JELLIED SALMON MOUSSE

The salmon skin and bones contain a generous amount of healthy oils. Use 'em!

1	15-ounce can red salmon, drain and reserve juice	1	medium onion, quartered
1½	envelopes unflavored gelatin	1	cup low fat yogurt
2	tablespoons lemon juice	½	cup lite mayonnaise
½	cup salmon juice	½	teaspoon paprika
		2	teaspoons dried dill weed (2 tablespoons fresh)

1. Soften gelatin in lemon juice for 5 minutes. Heat salmon juice to boiling. Add gelatin mixture to dissolve.

2. Process in food processor with steel blade for ½ minute. Add drained salmon and remaining ingredients and process until smooth.

3. Pour into greased 1 quart mold; chill 5 hours or overnight. A fish-shaped mold makes an attractive presentation.

4. Unmold on serving platter. Surround with cucumber slices.

For an interesting texture, flake ⅓ of salmon and fold in after completing step 2.

You may wish to accompany with CUCUMBER DILL SAUCE (Page 243).

YIELD: 4 cups

Nutritive Values (per tablespoon)		calories	25.0 kc
total fat	1.8 g	carbohydrates	0.4 g
monosaturated fat	0.5 g	fiber	trace g
polyunsaturated fat	0.9 g	protein	1.7 g
saturated fat	0.3 g	sodium	49.5 mg
cholesterol	1.2 mg	sugar	0.2 g

CRAB OR LOBSTER ASPIC

2	envelopes unflavored gelatin		Juice of 1 lemon
*½	cup cold chicken broth*	2	chopped sweet pickles
1	cup boiling chicken broth	*1	pound real or mock crab or lobster, chopped or shredded
½	to ¾ cup chili sauce		
	Salt to taste	1	cup diced celery

1. Soften gelatin in cold soup. Add hot soup and stir until dissolved. Cool.

2. Add lemon juice, chili sauce, and salt, if necessary. Chill slightly.

3. When mixture begins to thicken, add pickles, seafood, and celery.

4. Place in a greased 5 cup mold (a fish shaped mold makes an attractive presentation). Chill 4 to 6 hours or overnight.

Serve with plates and forks. Good with party rye, PITA TRIANGLES (Page 255) or crackers. Have a bowl of COCKTAIL SAUCE (Page 242) available to spoon over each serving.

*Use canned chicken broth or CHICKEN BROTH (Page 208)

**SPOTLIGHT (Page 95)

SPOTLIGHT *on preparing crabmeat: for crab dishes using canned or frozen crab, pick it over carefully for pieces of bone and shell.*

Nutritive values calculated using cooked lobster. Use low sodium chili sauce and chicken broth for reduced sodium content.

YIELD: 8 servings

Nutritive Values (per serving)			
		calories	91.5 kc
total fat	0.4 g	carbohydrates	6.5 g
monosaturated fat	trace	fiber	0.3 g
polyunsaturated fat	trace	protein	14.3 g
saturated fat	trace	sodium	585.0 mg
cholesterol	40.8 mg	sugar	0.2 g

GEFILTE FISH MOLD

Put cherry tomatoes in center of this tasty mold.

*1	24-ounce jar of gefilte fish in jellied broth (6-8 pieces)	1	cup boiling water
		1	cup reserved fish broth
		½	cup red horseradish
2	small packages lemon gelatin	1	tablespoon lemon juice

1. Drain fish, reserving broth.

2. Mix gelatin and boiling water; stir until dissolved.

3. Add remaining ingredients except fish.

4. Chill until partially set. Pour half of gelatin mixture into greased 2 quart ring mold. Place fish pieces carefully on top of gelatin. Pour remaining gelatin over all.

5. Chill overnight or until set.

Unmold on serving tray lined with radiccio or leaf lettuce.

Serve with plates and forks.

*See GEFILTE FISH (Page 110) for a quick and easy food processor method to make your own.

For a reduced calorie version use gelatin made with artificial sweetener.

YIELD: 9 servings

Nutritive Values (per serving)		calories	78.0 kc
total fat	1.5 g	carbohydrates	7.9 g
monosaturated fat	0.7 g	fiber	trace g
polyunsaturated fat	0.2 g	protein	7.9 g
saturated fat	0.4 g	sodium	601.0 mg
cholesterol	24.0 mg	sugar	0.2 g

LOX RING

1 envelope unflavored gelatin	6 ounces lox, dried on paper towel and coarsely chopped
¼ cup cold water	Dash white pepper
*3 cups low-fat yogurt, drained 24 hours	¼ cup chopped fresh parsley (2 tablespoons dried parsley)
2 tablespoons sherry	
¾ teaspoon seasoned salt	Parsley and green pepper for garnish
1 2-ounce jar pimientos, sliced and drained	

1. Sprinkle cold water over gelatin and stir to dissolve. Melt over hot water to dissolve completely.

2. Beat gelatin into yogurt in electric mixer or food processor.

3. Stir in remaining ingredients.

4. Pour into 3 cup ring mold. Refrigerate until set, 4 hours or overnight.

5. Turn out onto a plate and garnish with fresh parsley and green pepper slices.

Serve sliced with forks and little plates along with a variety of small crisp crackers or party rye.

*ALL ABOUT YOGURT (Page 154)

YIELD: 12 servings

Nutritive Values (per serving)		calories	60.0 kc
total fat	1.5 g	carbohydrates	4.7 g
monosaturated fat	0.5 g	fiber	trace
polyunsaturated fat	0.1 g	protein	6.1 g
saturated fat	0.7 g	sodium	285.4 mg
cholesterol	6.7 mg	sugar	3.0 g

FISH TERRINE-21st CENTURY

We've taken the fat out of this dish by substituting evaporated skim milk for the traditional heavy cream. Do it quickly in your food processor and get the same light texture that chefs achieve with much more work!

1 pound fresh halibut or scrod, cut into 2-inch cubes	2 tablespoons dill weed (2 teaspoons dried)
2 egg whites	A few grinds of pepper
2 tablespoons chopped fresh parsley	4 drops Tabasco
½ teaspoon salt	1½ cups evaporated skim milk, undiluted

ALL INGREDIENTS MUST BE VERY COLD

1. Using steel knife, chop fish in food processor until consistency of smooth paste. Add egg whites, parsley, dill weed, and seasonings and continue processing for ½ minute.

2. With food processor running, gradually add sufficient chilled evaporated skim milk to form a thick paste.

3. Grease a 1 quart loaf pan or ring mold. Spoon in fish mixture, tapping pan to eliminate air bubbles. Cover tightly with a piece of greased aluminum foil.

4. Place in deep pan. Pour in boiling water to reach halfway up sides of pan of fish. Bake in preheated 350° oven for 45 minutes until fish feels springy but firm in center.

5. Take out of oven and cool for 10 minutes. Loosen around edges with table knife and invert on serving platter. Slice thinly. Serve with plates and forks.

Serve warm with LOBSTER SAUCE (Page 246) or cold with CUCUMBER DILL SAUCE (Page 243) or with your favorite Thousand Island dressing.

YIELD: 10 servings

Nutritive Values (per serving)		calories	79.0 kc
total fat	0.7 g	carbohydrates	4.5 g
monosaturated fat	0.1 g	fiber	trace
polyunsaturated fat	0.2 g	protein	13.0 g
saturated fat	0.2 g	sodium	191.0 mg
cholesterol	18.0 mg	sugar	trace

HERRING AND BEETS

A colorful change of pace herring

1	16-ounce can red beets, drained	1	hard cooked egg, white only
2	16-ounce jars of herring in wine sauce, drained	1	large dill pickle
		1	medium apple, unpeeled
1	6-ounce can potatoes, drained, or 1 cup boiled potatoes	*1	cup low fat yogurt, drained 1 hour
		1/3	cup chopped almonds
		1	tablespoon sugar

1. Cut first six ingredients into small cubes.

2. Mix yogurt with sugar and almonds; add to salad and mix well.

Place in a salad bowl. Serve with slices of rye bread.

*ALL ABOUT YOGURT (Page 154)

SPOTLIGHT *is brilliant when it instructs us to rinse salt herring with water and pat dry with paper towels. Don't get hooked on salt!*

To reduce sodium, rinse herring with cold water and drain on paper towel. Omit dill pickle.

YIELD: 15 ½-cup servings

Nutritive Values (per serving)		calories	211.0 kc
total fat	12.7 g	carbohydrates	13.5 g
monosaturated fat	8.3 g	fiber	1.1 g
polyunsaturated fat	1.4 g	protein	10.6 g
saturated fat	1.7 g	sodium	689.0 mg
cholesterol	8.8 mg	sugar	5.0 g

GEFILTE FISH

Don't let Grandma tell you how hard she worked chopping Gefilte fish. With a food processor, it is a 5 minute job.

2	carrots, cut into thick slices	½	pound pike fillet (skin removed)
2	tablespoons sugar	2	medium onions
1	onion	1	teaspoon salt
2	pounds fish heads and bones	2	tablespoons matzo meal or cracker crumbs
2	stalks celery and leaves	⅛	teaspoon fresh ground pepper
3	sprigs parsley	1½	teaspoons sugar
1	teaspoon salt	1	large egg
½	pound whitefish fillet (skin removed)		

1. Place first 7 ingredients in large soup pot with water to cover generously. Bring to a boil and simmer one hour.

2. While stock is boiling, chill fish in freezer for 15 minutes. Place fish in food processor bowl with steel blade.

3. Process for 1 minute; scrape down sides of bowl and process an additional half minute.

4. Add remaining ingredients. Process 1 minute; scrape down sides of bowl and process 1 minute longer or until smooth consistency. (The mixture should hold its shape when dropped from a spoon.)

5. Chill in refrigerator for 1 hour.

GEFILTE FISH *(continued)*

6. Shape into balls. Place carefully on top of bones and vegetables in soup pot of boiling broth.

7. Return to a boil, reduce heat, cover pot and simmer 1 hour. Shake pan occasionally, gently, but do not stir.

8. Remove cooked fish balls carefully to a bowl. Strain the broth over them. Add cooked carrots to bowl of fish.

9. Chill until broth jells. For a thicker broth, add 1 teaspoon gelatin that has been softened in 2 tablespoons cold water and then dissolved in 1 cup of the boiling broth.

Note that only a part of the evaluated sodium in this recipe is absorbed by the finished product.

YIELD: 20 pieces			
Nutritive Values (per piece)		calories	45.0 kc
total fat	0.6 g	carbohydrates	4.3 g
monosaturated fat	0.2 g	fiber	0.7 g
polyunsaturated fat	0.8 g	protein	5.3 g
saturated fat	0.2 g	sodium	238.0 mg
cholesterol	19.0 mg	sugar	2.2 g

SMOKY SALMON LOG

1   1-pound can salmon
¼   teaspoon salt
2   teaspoons grated
      onion
*1⅔ cups low-fat yogurt,
      drained 24 hours
      and patted dry on
      paper towels
¼   teaspoon liquid smoke

1   tablespoon lemon
      juice
1   teaspoon prepared
      horseradish
3   tablespoons snipped
      parsley
½   cup chopped walnuts
      (optional)

1. Drain salmon well.

2. Blend with next 6 ingredients in food processor.

3. Shape into log.

4. Roll log in nuts and parsley, or just in parsley.

5. Chill until firm (4-5 hours or overnight).

Serve with party rye bread.

*ALL ABOUT YOGURT (Page 154)

YIELD: 2½ cups

Nutritive Values (per tablespoon)		calories	31.0 kc
total fat	1.8 g	carbohydrates	1.0 g
monosaturated fat	0.8 g	fiber	0.1 g
polyunsaturated fat	0.5 g	protein	2.8 g
saturated fat	0.3 g	sodium	84.4 mg
cholesterol	0.6 mg	sugar	0.6 g

SALMON PÂTÉ

Impress your guests with this scrumptous spread!

1	cup dry white wine	1	pound fresh salmon fillets
6	peppercorns		
2	bay leaves	1/3	cup margarine
4	sprigs dill weed or 1 teaspoon dried	1/2	teaspoon lemon pepper
4	sprigs cilantro or parsley		Thinly sliced cucumber for garnish
2	tablespoons fresh lemon juice	2	tablespoons chopped fresh dill weed or 2 teaspoons dried
2	tablespoons dehydrated onion		
1	clove minced garlic	1	tablespoon capers

1. Simmer first 8 ingredients for 5 minutes in large covered skillet. Let stand 10 minutes; strain.

2. Poach salmon over low heat in strained liquid for 5 minutes. Remove from heat and leave in poaching liquid for 10 minutes.

3. Take salmon from pan; drain on paper towel and flake with a fork; mix in margarine and lemon pepper.

4. Pack firmly into bowl that has been lined with plastic wrap. Refrigerate. To unmold, lift out of bowl on to serving tray.

Garnish with cucumber slices, capers and dill weed. Serve with party rye or crackers. Try our CARAWAY RYE CRISPS (Page 254).

VARIATION: RED SNAPPER PÂTÉ:
Substitute 1 pound red snapper for the salmon.

YIELD: 2 cups			
Nutritive Values (per tablespoon)		calories	39.0 kc
total fat	2.3 g	carbohydrates	0.3 g
monosaturated fat	0.7 g	fiber	trace
polyunsaturated fat	1.1 g	protein	2.6 g
saturated fat	0.3 g	sodium	34.3 mg
cholesterol	7.5 mg	sugar	0.1 g

SEAFOOD-FILLED ARTICHOKE BOTTOMS

Elegant and easy

*1 6-ounce can crabmeat or 6 ounces mock crab, flaked
2 teaspoons thinly sliced green onion stems
1 tablespoon lite mayonnaise
6 artichoke bottoms
   Capers or parsley
6 tiny wedges of sliced lemon

1. Mix drained crabmeat with mayonnaise and onion stems.

2. Place on top of drained artichoke bottoms.

3. Garnish each with capers or parsley and a lemon wedge.

You may wish to try mock lobster as an alternative.

*SPOTLIGHT (Pages 95, 105)

YIELD: 6 servings			
Nutritive Values (per serving)		calories	31.8 kc
total fat	0.9 g	carbohydrates	2.5 g
monosaturated fat	trace	fiber	trace
polyunsaturated fat	trace	protein	3.5 g
saturated fat	trace	sodium	0.2 mg
cholesterol	0.8 mg	sugar	0.1 g

CRAB MEAT FLORIDA

½ cup catsup
1-2 tablespoons prepared
    horseradish
1   teaspoon lemon juice
    Few drops Tabasco

*½ pound flaked crab
    meat or mock crab
    Pink grapefruit
    sections for garnish
    (optional)

Combine first 4 ingredients. Add crabmeat.

Line serving platter with lettuce. Spoon crabmeat mixture in center. Garnish with pink grapefruit sections.

Serve with crackers.

May also be served in individual compote dishes as crab cocktail.

*SPOTLIGHT (Pages 95, 105)

VARIATION: Add 1-2 tablespoons mayonnaise.

To reduce sodium, use low sodium catsup.

YIELD: 1½ cups			
Nutritive Values (per tablespoon)		calories	15.0 kc
total fat	0.1 g	carbohydrates	2.4 g
monosaturated fat	0.0 g	fiber	0.1 g
polyunsaturated fat	0.0 g	protein	1.1 g
saturated fat	0.0 g	sodium	138.0 mg
cholesterol	1.9 mg	sugar	0.6 g

SEAFOOD ALMOND BOATS

12 hard boiled eggs, halved. Discard yolk.	2 tablespoons minced green pepper
½ pound shredded crabmeat or mock crabmeat	1½ tablespoons drained low fat yogurt
½ cup minced celery	1½ tablespoons lite mayonnaise
¼ cup chopped almonds	1 teaspoon prepared mustard

Combine all ingredients except egg whites. Stuff egg white halves (see EGG BOATS below). Garnish (see below).

GENERAL INSTRUCTIONS FOR EGG BOATS

1. Pierce one end of egg with a pin to prevent cracking; place gently in saucepan; cover with cold water.
2. Bring to boil; reduce heat to keep water simmering and continue to cook for 15 minutes. Pour off boiling water and *immediately* let cold tap water run over eggs until cool enough to handle.
3. Remove shell and slice egg in half, lengthwise or crosswise. Discard egg yolk. (Feed it to the dog!) To make crosswise EGG BOATS stand on platter, trim a small slice of egg white from rounded end.
4. Prepare a day or two ahead: wrap airtight with plastic; store in refrigerator. Add garnish before serving.

OTHER FILLINGS

HUMMUS BI TIHINI (Page 149)
MUSTARD MADNESS (Page 152)
TUNA WHIP (Page 169)

GARNISHES

Paprika
Curry powder
Olive slice
Pimiento strip
Caper

YIELD: 24 pieces

Nutritive Values (per piece)		calories	21.9 kc
total fat	1.2 g	carbohydrates	0.8 g
monosaturated fat	0.6 g	fiber	0.2 g
polyunsaturated fat	0.4 g	protein	2.1 g
saturated fat	0.1 g	sodium	36.4 mg
cholesterol	0.1 mg	sugar	0.2 g

DOUGH EASY
phyllo, tortillas and crêpes

PHYLLO PASTRY

Phyllo is a paper-thin sheet of pastry, typically used in Middle Eastern countries. Readily available in frozen food cases of supermarkets, it permits easy preparation of Greek hors d'oeuvres.

GENERAL INSTRUCTIONS

With reasonable care, phyllo is relatively easy to work with. The following precautions and suggestions will be helpful:

1. To prevent stickiness from condensation or excessive drying and cracking, thaw frozen phyllo pastry in the refrigerator overnight. Set the closed box of pastry out at room temperature for two hours before use.

2. For ease in handling, remove dough from package, cover with sheet of waxed paper and damp towel. Uncover only the sheet of pastry you are using.

3. Phyllo sheets may tear, but can be patched easily with another piece of dough.

4. Use a very sharp knife for cutting and slicing.

5. Each sheet of pastry must be lightly greased for crispness and to prevent drying or cracking.

6. Individual pastries should be filled with a filling of fairly thick consistency. Since they expand when baking they should not be overstuffed or wrapped too tightly.

7. Before baking recipe topped with phyllo pastry, grease the top crust, score into serving pieces and cut through top three or four layers of the pastry with sharp knife. After baking, cut on these lines to serve.

8. Cool pastries on wire rack for 10 minutes before serving.

9. Unused phyllo, well wrapped, will keep for a month in refrigerator.

10. Prepared pastries can be frozen before baking. Freeze individual pastries in a single layer on a wax paper lined pan. When solid, place in airtight container. (Allow extra baking time.)

CRAB PHYLLO HORS D'OEUVRE

We've reduced saturated fat, cholesterol and calories by replacing the traditional butter with olive oil spray. Read page 119 for general instructions on handling phyllo dough.

1 cup skim milk	***3 tablespoons chopped almonds, toasted
2 tablespoons dry sherry	Salt and pepper to taste
*Instant blend flour	9 phyllo leaves
**2 cans crab meat or 8 ounces mock crab, coarsely chopped	Olive oil spray

1. Mix sherry and milk. Bring to boil; add flour to thicken. Add chopped almonds and crabmeat. Correct seasoning.

2. Grease a 9x13 inch pan lightly with margarine.

3. Spray 4 phyllo leaves lightly with olive oil. Layer them into pan. Spread filling over phyllo.

4. Prepare 5 additional phyllo leaves; place over filling. Trim even with top edge of pan. With sharp knife, score through top leaves to mark slices. Spray top lightly with olive oil. Bake at 400° for 15 minutes. Reduce oven to 350° and continue baking for another 15 minutes.

5. Place on wire rack for 10 minutes. While still warm, cut into 1½-inch squares.

*SPOTLIGHT (Page 94)

**SPOTLIGHT (Pages 95, 105)

***SPOTLIGHT (Page 151)

YIELD: 35 pieces

Nutritive Values (per piece)		calories	24.0 kc
total fat	0.6 g	carbohydrates	3.7 g
monosaturated fat	0.4 g	fiber	trace g
polyunsaturated fat	trace	protein	0.9 g
saturated fat	trace	sodium	36.0 mg
cholesterol	0.1 mg	sugar	0.4 g

♥ CHICKEN PHYLLO APPETIZERS

1   recipe BASIC GROUND POULTRY MIX (Page 17)
3   tablespoons taco sauce (fire eaters use
    hot taco sauce)
    Olive oil spray
    Seasoned salt (optional)
8   sheets phyllo dough

1. Add taco sauce to poultry mix.

2. Lay out 2 phyllo sheets; spray each lightly with olive oil, going to edges. Cut lengthwise into 6 strips with scissors or very sharp knife.

3. Place 1 tablespoon of filling at end of each strip. Fold over one corner to opposite side to make a triangle. Continue folding, keeping triangle shape to the end of the strip. (See attached drawing.) Repeat until all filling is used.

4. Put filled triangles on ungreased cookie sheet. Spray lightly with oil. Sprinkle with seasoned salt. Bake 20 minutes at 350° or until golden brown, turning once after 10 minutes. Cool 5 minutes on wire rack before serving.

Pass extra taco sauce for dipping.

You can make and bake the day before. Refrigerate covered; reheat at 350°, uncovered on a cookie sheet, until thoroughly heated.

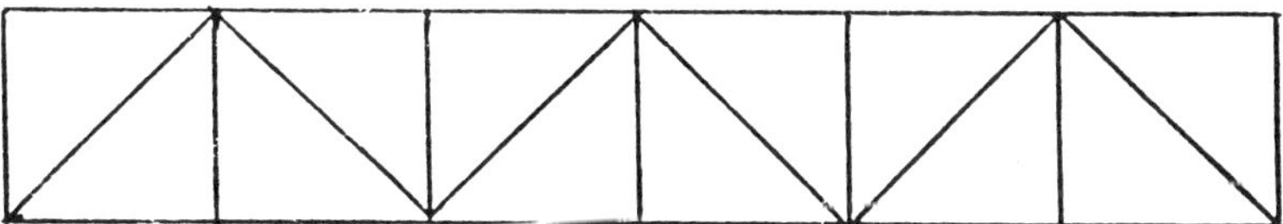

YIELD: 24 pieces

Nutritive Values (per piece)		calories	57.3 kc
total fat	2.3 g	carbohydrates	5.1 g
monosaturated fat	0.8 g	fiber	0.0 g
polyunsaturated fat	0.8 g	protein	4.3 g
saturated fat	0.6 g	sodium	79.7 mg
cholesterol	13.9 mg	sugar	0.1 g

CHICKEN TORTILLA ROLL

*1   pound thinly sliced
      mushrooms
2   teaspoons margarine
½   recipe BASIC
      GROUND POULTRY
      MIX (Page 17)
2   teaspoons Parmesan
½   teaspoon salt

⅛   teaspoon freshly
      ground pepper
¾   cup skim milk
**1-2 tablespoons instant
      blend flour
3   10-inch flour tortillas
8   ounces shredded part
      skim milk mozzarella
      Corn oil spray

1. Sauté mushrooms in margarine in nonstick saucepan until limp. Stir in Parmesan, salt and pepper. Add milk; heat to boiling. Add enough instant blend flour to thicken; cool.

2. Blend poultry mix into mushrooms.

3. Place ⅓ of mushroom mixture on lower third of first tortilla. Place 2 tablespoons of mozzarella on top edge. Roll into cylinder, starting at filling end. Repeat with remaining tortillas.

4. Place on greased baking sheet, seam side down. Spray lightly with oil.

5. Bake at 350° for 20 minutes. Spread remaining cheese on top of rolls. Return to oven and continue baking until cheese melts. Allow to rest for 5 minutes. Cut into 1 inch slices with kitchen scissors or very sharp knife.

For a spicy touch, serve with a bowl of PLUM TOMATO SALSA (Page 240).

*SPOTLIGHT (Pages 59, 71)

**SPOTLIGHT (Page 94)

YIELD: 30 slices			
Nutritive Values (per slice)		calories	56.3 kc
total fat	2.9 g	carbohydrates	3.5 g
monosaturated fat	0.8 g	fiber	0.2 g
polyunsaturated fat	0.7 g	protein	4.2 g
saturated fat	1.1 g	sodium	99.7 mg
cholesterol	10.1 mg	sugar	0.6 g

CHIMICHANGAS

Go south of the border with leftover chicken or turkey!

2½ cups shredded cooked chicken or turkey
⅔ cup picante sauce or salsa
⅓ cup sliced scallions
1-2 teaspoons chili powder
¼ teaspoon salt
8 7- or 8-inch flour tortillas
Olive oil spray
1 cup (4 ounces) shredded lite cheddar or Monterey Jack cheese

1. Combine first 5 ingredients in saucepan; simmer until most of liquid has evaporated.

2. Spray top side of tortillas with olive oil.

3. Spoon ⅓ cup filling in center of sprayed tortilla; top with 2 tablespoons cheese. Fold 2 sides over filling; fold in ends. Place seam side down in baking dish.

4. Bake in preheated 475° oven 12-14 minutes until golden brown.

Serve with plates and forks. Pass drained low fat yogurt and additional picante sauce.

Nutritive values do not include toppings. To reduce sodium, use low sodium picante sauce and omit salt.

YIELD: 8 servings			
Nutritive Values (per serving)		calories	300.8 kc
total fat	10.9 g	carbohydrates	20.2 g
monosaturated fat	3.2 g	fiber	0.3 g
polyunsaturated fat	1.4 g	protein	29.6 g
saturated fat	3.3 g	sodium	195.9 mg
cholesterol	73.7 mg	sugar	0.6 g

CRÊPES

Crêpe is the French word for a thin, delicate pancake which forms the basis for many delicious entrées, tempting appetizers, and desserts. They can be used for a brunch, luncheon, elegant dinner party or at any gathering that you want to be a little different and very special. The crêpe may be seasoned and filled and then rolled, folded or stacked. Fillings for crêpes can be fish, meat, poultry, vegetables, cheese, or whatever strikes your fancy. Be daring — use your imagination! These fillings are a wonderful way to make use of leftovers.

GENERAL INSTRUCTIONS FOR CRÊPES

BASIC CRÊPE RECIPE

⅛	teaspoon salt	1	cup flour
3	egg beaters or	2	tablespoons melted
	3 egg whites plus		margarine
	1 tablespoon	1¼	cups skim milk
	margarine		

MIXING THE CRÊPES

1. Place flour and salt in a 4 cup measure.

2. Add eggs and shortening and stir with a wire whisk until just blended.

3. Gradually add milk and continue stirring with wire whisk until there are no lumps. Don't overbeat or the crêpes will be tough. If there are some lumps pour through a strainer.

4. Allow batter to stand at least 1 hour or overnight before making crêpes. This allows the flour to absorb the liquid. If the batter becomes too thick after standing, a little liquid may be added; it should be the consistency of light cream.

BAKING THE CRÊPES

1. Heat the seasoned crêpe pan or skillet until it is hot enough that a few drops of water sprinkled on the surface dance into small beads. IT IS CRUCIAL THAT THE PAN BE HOT WHEN THE BATTER IS POURED.

CRÊPES *(continued)*

2. Brush the pan with a small amount of melted margarine. Margarine should not brown.

3. Lift pan off heat. Pour batter into pan (2 or 3 tablespoons for a 6-inch pan). Immediately tilt and turn the pan so the bottom is completely covered with the batter. Any excess can be poured out.

4. Place pan back on heat and continue cooking for 1-2 minutes or until lightly browned and blistered.

5. Turn crêpe and cook on second side if so stated in the recipe instructions. Second side will brown in 30 seconds.

6. Slide the finished crêpes onto a tea towel. Stack when cool. This helps soften the edges and facilitates folding or rolling.

7. If recipe suggests keeping crêpes warm, cover with a piece of aluminum foil and put in a 200° oven.

8. To store crêpes, put in a plastic bag and refrigerate up to 4 days, or freeze up to 2 months.

9. To reheat crêpes, brush a baking sheet or heatproof dish with melted margarine. Peel off the crêpes and lay them overlapping on baking sheet. Brush them lightly with melted margarine to protect them while heating and bake in a 400° oven just long enough to heat.

From BEGINNING AGAIN, MORE HORS D'OEUVRES, Rockdale Ridge Press, 1981.

YIELD: 24 crêpes

Nutritive Values (per crêpe)		calories	38.0 kc
total fat	1.5 g	carbohydrates	4.6 g
monosaturated fat	0.4 g	fiber	0.1 g
polyunsaturated fat	0.8 g	protein	1.4 g
saturated fat	0.2 g	sodium	46.0 mg
cholesterol	0.2 mg	sugar	0.7 g

CRÊPES (continued)

THE CRÊPE PAN

The right pan is very important for making perfect crêpes. It should be small, usually 6 to 9 inches in diameter. It should have rounded sides. It is essential to use a good quality pan...heavy, but not so heavy that it cannot be lifted to swirl the batter. There are a number of new and interesting crêpe pans and electric crêpe makers on the market which are fun and easy to use. Teflon is good for beginners as it is easy to use and the crêpes do not stick. Ideally the pan should be kept only for making crêpes and should be properly seasoned.

SEASONING THE CRÊPE PAN

Follow the manufacturer's recommendations for seasoning or other treatment of the pan. If there are no instructions use this method:

Pour vegetable oil into the bottom of the pan covering the entire surface. Heat until the oil is very hot and begins to smoke. Let the oil stand in the pan, off the heat, overnight. Pour out the oil and wipe clean with paper towels.

CLEANING THE PAN

To clean the pan NEVER WASH WITH SOAP AND WATER, wipe out with a paper towel. If it is necessary to wash the pan, cure it again before using.

BLINTZES

1 recipe BASIC CRÊPES (Page 124)

12 ounces uncreamed cottage cheese or baker's cheese

2 egg beaters or 2 egg whites

½ teaspoon grated lemon rind

¼ teaspoon cinnamon (optional)

2 teaspoons sugar

¼ teaspoon salt

1 teaspoon melted margarine

1. Follow general instructions for mixing and baking crêpes. Cook crêpe on one side only until it blisters and is lightly browned. Place finished crêpe on a tea towel, brown side up.

2. Mix filling ingredients in food processor until well blended and smooth, using steel blade.

3. Place 1 to 1½ tablespoons filling in the center of the crêpe. Fold as an envelope.

4. Heat 1 teaspoon margarine in a nonstick skillet. Place blintzes in skillet, seam side down. Fry on both sides to a golden brown. Add more margarine sparingly as necessary.

5. Blintzes may also be baked on a greased pan in a 350° oven. Place on pan, seam side down. Brush with melted margarine. They must be turned once.

Serve with low fat yogurt and preserves.

Nutritive values calculated using egg whites.

YIELD: 16 blintzes

Nutritive Values (per crêpe)		calories	74.0 kc
total fat	0.4 g	carbohydrates	10.0 g
monosaturated fat	trace	fiber	0.2 g
polyunsaturated fat	trace	protein	5.9 g
saturated fat	trace	sodium	191.0 mg
cholesterol	1.7 mg	sugar	3.7 g

 CANNELONI

This heart signifies one of our very best cocktail-buffet recipes: crêpes filled with spinach and ground poultry, bathed with scrumptuous sauces and Parmesan cheese. This is a great way to enhance your leftover Thanksgiving turkey.

CRÊPES:

Follow GENERAL INSTRUCTIONS FOR CRÊPES (BASIC CRÊPE RECIPE, Page 124). Brown on one side only. Place on tea towel, brown side down.

TOMATO SAUCE:

1   10½-ounce can spaghetti sauce
1   15-ounce can tomato sauce

Combine tomato sauce ingredients. Set aside.

BÉCHAMEL SAUCE:

2	tablespoons margarine	2	cups skim milk
2	tablespoons instant blend flour	½	cup shredded part skim mozzarella

1. Melt margarine in top of double boiler; blend in flour.

2. Gradually add milk, beating with a wire whisk until smooth. Heat over boiling water, stirring constantly until thickened.

3. Add cheese and stir until blended.

FILLING:

½	cup chopped mushrooms	2	cups chopped cooked turkey or chicken breast
2	scallions, chopped		
1	tablespoon margarine	4	lightly beaten egg whites
2	10-ounce packages frozen spinach		Salt or salt substitute to taste
1	stick cinnamon		
⅔	cup seasoned bread crumbs	⅛	teaspoon pepper
			Dash nutmeg
3	tablespoons chopped parsley or 1 tablespoon dried	4	ounces chopped lean ham
		⅛	teaspoon thyme
		½	cup grated Parmesan

CANNELONI *(continued)*

1. Sauté mushrooms and scallions in margarine.

2. Cook spinach with cinnamon stick; drain and discard cinnamon and squeeze spinach dry.

3. Combine all filling ingredients, reserving ¼ cup Parmesan.

ASSEMBLY:

1. Grease a 10×14 inch bake and serve pan or paella pan.

2. Cover bottom of pan with ¾ cup tomato sauce.

3. Spread each crêpe with 2 tablespoons filling, leaving a ½ inch border all around. Roll into cylinders.

4. Arrange in prepared baking pan, seam side down. Cover with remaining tomato sauce. Top with Béchamel sauce. Sprinkle with remaining ¼ cup Parmesan cheese.

5. Bake 30 minutes at 350° until hot and bubbling.

Prepare in advance and heat when ready to serve.

To reduce sodium, substitute low sodium spaghetti sauce and tomato sauce. To reduce fat and cholesterol content, use only one half the Parmesan.

YIELD: 24 crêpes

Nutritive Values (per crêpe)		calories	138.0 kc
total fat	4.1 g	carbohydrates	13.5 g
monosaturated fat	1.3 g	fiber	1.0 g
polyunsaturated fat	1.3 g	protein	11.9 g
saturated fat	0.9 g	sodium	381.0 mg
cholesterol	20.9 mg	sugar	1.7 g

CRABMEAT CRÊPES

1 recipe BASIC CRÊPES (Page 124)
1 cup skim milk
½ cup chicken broth, fat removed
    Salt and pepper
*3 tablespoons instant blend flour
1 tablespoon grated Parmesan
2 tablespoons sherry

½ cup sliced water chestnuts
**¾ cup crabmeat or mock crab
1 small jar pimientos, drained and sliced
15 stalks of asparagus, canned or fresh, cooked
    Extra Parmesan

CRÊPES: make according to general directions, browning on one side.

CRAB SAUCE: combine milk and chicken broth in saucepan. Heat to boiling and add flour, stirring until thickened. Remove from heat. Add salt and pepper to taste. Stir in remaining ingredients, except asparagus.

ASSEMBLING CRÊPES: lay one stalk of asparagus on each crêpe. Spread with 1½ tablespoons crab sauce. Roll in cylinders. Place in a greased bake and serve dish, seam side down. Sprinkle with Parmesan.

BAKING CRÊPES: bake at 300° for 30 minutes or until heated through.

Serve with remaining crab sauce.

Prepare in advance and heat before serving.

*SPOTLIGHT (Page 94)

**SPOTLIGHT (Pages 95, 105)

YIELD: 15 crêpes			
Nutritive Values (per crêpe)		calories	75.0 kc
total fat	1.1 g	carbohydrates	1.5 g
monosaturated fat	0.3 g	fiber	0.9 g
polyunsaturated fat	0.2 g	protein	1.8 g
saturated fat	0.5 g	sodium	121.4 mg
cholesterol	1.9 mg	sugar	1.9 g

CRÊPES RATATOUILLE

1	recipe BASIC CRÊPES (Page 124)	1	8-ounce can tomato sauce
1	small eggplant, peeled and chopped or shredded	1	tablespoon sugar (optional)
3	medium zucchini, chopped or shredded	¼	teaspoon basil
		¼	teaspoon thyme
2	tablespoons olive oil	2	tablespoons parsley, chopped
1	large onion, chopped		Salt to taste
½	green pepper, chopped		Pepper to taste
1	16-ounce can tomatoes, drained and chopped	2	cups (8 ounces) shredded part skim milk mozzarella

1. Make crêpes according to general directions (Page 124). Brown on one side only.

2. Sauté eggplant and zucchini in nonstick skillet in 1 tablespoon oil until vegetables are soft. If there is excess liquid in the pan, drain. Set aside.

3. Sauté onion and green pepper in remaining oil. Mix with remaining ingredients except cheese. Simmer for 30 minutes or until sauce thickens; add zucchini and eggplant mixture.

4. Place about 2 tablespoons of vegetable mixture on unbrowned side of a crêpe. Roll up and place in a greased casserole, seam side down.

5. Pour remaining filling over all crêpes in casserole and sprinkle with mozzarella cheese.

6. Bake in a 350° oven for about 15 minutes or until crêpes are hot and cheese melted.

To reduce fat and cholesterol, use only 1 cup mozzarella.

YIELD: 20 crêpes

Nutritive Values (per piece)		calories	87.4 kc
total fat	3.4 g	carbohydrates	9.6 g
monosaturated fat	1.5 g	fiber	1.1 g
polyunsaturated fat	0.2 g	protein	4.9 g
saturated fat	1.4 g	sodium	266.3 mg
cholesterol	6.7 mg	sugar	2.4 g

ASPARAGUS WONDER

1   recipe BASIC CRÊPES (Page 124)
24 stalks asparagus (medium width)
½ cup MOCK BOURSIN AU POIVRE (Page 156)

1. Prepare crêpes according to general directions, browning on both sides. Cool; cut each crêpe in half.

2. Cook asparagus until tender crisp; drain on paper towels.

3. Spread each crêpe half with cheese and top with one piece of asparagus, the tip end extending ½ inch over the edge of the crêpe. Roll up.

Serve at room temperature.

YIELD: 24 crêpes

Nutritive Values (per crêpe)		calories	35.0 kc
total fat	0.3 g	carbohydrates	6.0 g
monosaturated fat	trace	fiber	0.4 g
polyunsaturated fat	trace	protein	2.2 g
saturated fat	0.1 g	sodium	106.0 mg
cholesterol	0.8 mg	sugar	1.3 g

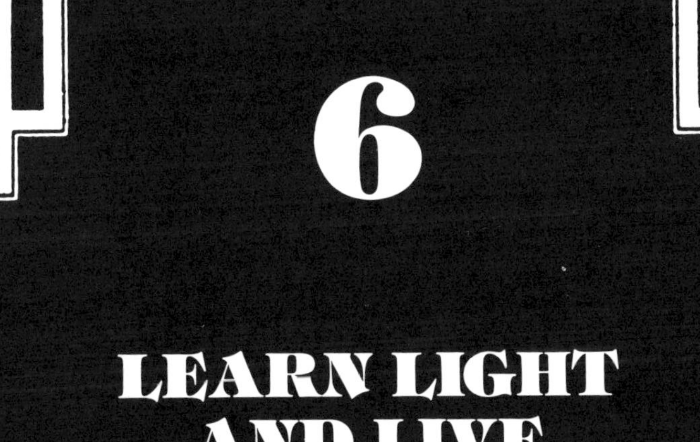
6

LEARN LIGHT
AND LIVE
comparisons and
substitutions

LEARN LIGHT AND LIVE

BEGINNING LIGHT advises, "Eat, drink and be wary." There is no need to feel deprived of tasty food when you give careful attention to nutritive values on product labels. A trip through the grocery store reveals a broad spectrum of delicious foods that limit cholesterol, reduce total fat and avoid harmful fats and oils.

ABOUT PRODUCT LABEL READING

BEGINNING LIGHT is precise when it focuses on discerning nutritive label reading. The nutritive label lists first, the ingredients present in greatest quantity. Labels may be misleading. Products labeled "no cholesterol" or "100% vegetable oil" may indeed contain harmful vegetable oils. Labels are a map to better health. Learn to read them!

The diverse nutritional requirements of your family's dietary needs can be met with a single set of meals if thoughtfully planned. It is easy to convert favorite dishes from high fat, high cholesterol products into heart healthy treats. Appropriate substitutions can be accomplished without destroying the character, flavor and identity of the dish. Eliminate hidden fats while you fool the eye and the palate.

Data for charts and tables was derived from DIET SIMPLE PLUS™ data base and/or manufacturer's package labels.

MAKE MODERATION, NOT DEPRIVATION YOUR KEYNOTE FOR THE 90'S.

Some food groups tend to raise cholesterol levels. Try to adhere to the following suggestions.

AVOID:

EXCESSIVE SATURATED FAT INTAKE

Foods containing significant amounts of saturated fat are: butter, 2% or whole milk, high fat cheeses, palm oil, palm kernel oil, coconut oil, hydrogenated vegetable oils and animal fats.

EXCESSIVE TOTAL FAT INTAKE

Even the "good" fats and oils must be limited.

EXCESSIVE CHOLESTEROL INTAKE

Limit meat, cheese and fish to a total of 6 ounces per day. Limit egg yolks according to your physician's advice.

DO EAT:

WATER SOLUBLE FIBER

Foods containing generous amounts of water soluble fiber are: legumes, bran, apples, apricots prunes, broccoli, cabbage, carrots, corn, peas and unpeeled potatoes.

ABOUT SUBSTITUTIONS

Substitute:
- Skim milk for 2% or whole milk
- Tub or squeeze margarines for butter or stick margarine
- Egg whites or egg substitutes for whole eggs
- Drained low fat or non fat yogurt for sour cream, cream cheese or whole milk yogurt
- Pasta made without egg yolks for egg noodles or pasta

Polyunsaturated and monounsaturated oils for palm, palm kernel, coconut, animal fats and hydrogenated vegetable oils

Vegetable oil sprays for solid vegetable shortenings and animal fats

Ground lean poultry for ground beef

ABOUT COMPLEX CARBOHYDRATES

Foods containing generous amounts of complex carbohydrates are:

Pasta and noodles made without egg yolks
Grains, rice
Cereals made without palm, palm kernel and coconut oils
Breads containing less than 2 grams of fat per serving
Fruits and vegetables

MARGARINE, COOKING OIL AND MAYONNAISE

Be aware that margarines, cooking oils and mayonnaises, even those containing beneficial polyunsaturated and monounsaturated oils, are high in calories. Include them in your diet in limited amounts.

ABOUT MARGARINE

Squeeze or tub margarines as opposed to stick products, are usually your healthier choice. *Liquid vegetable oil should be the first ingredient* listed on the product's nutritive label. Stick margarines listing *hydrogenated vegetable oils* among the first ingredients are not as healthy. Look for a P:S ratio of at least 2:1, twice as much polyunsaturated fat as saturated fat. (P:S is the ratio of polyunsaturates to saturated fats.)

Check also for cholesterol content. Margarines made with butter will contain cholesterol.

COMPARISON CHART: MARGARINES

Brand	Type	P:S Ratio	Cholesterol
Fleischman's	Squeeze	5:1	0 mg
Promise	Tub	5:1	0 mg
Promise Extra Light	Tub	3:1	0 mg
Fleischman's Soft	Tub	5:2	0 mg
Fleischmann's	Stick	4:2	0 mg
I Can't Believe It's Not Butter	Squeeze	4:2	0 mg
Mazola	Stick	4:2	0 mg
Promise	Stick	2:1	0 mg
Fleischmann's Light	Tub	3:2	0 mg
I Can't Believe It's Not Butter	Stick	2:2	0 mg
Land O' Lakes Country Morning	Stick	1:1	5 mg
Parkay	Stick	1:2	0 mg

Data derived from manufactuerer's package labels.

ABOUT COOKING OIL

Avoid coconut, palm, palm kernel, hydrogenated vegetable oils and animal fats. Hydrogenated shortenings, those that remain solid at room temperature, are not good choices. Instead, choose healthy vegetable oils: canola, corn, olive, peanut, safflower, sesame, soybean, partially hydrogenated vegetable and walnut oils.

There is evidence that oils such as canola and olive oil, containing generous amounts of monounsaturated fats, may be beneficial.

COMPARISON CHART: COOKING OILS

	Polyunsaturated	Saturated	Cholesterol
Canola	4	1	0
Corn	4	1	0
Olive	2	1	0
Peanut	4	2	0
Safflower	11	1	0
Sesame			
Soybean			
Sunflower	5	1	0
Vegetable	4	1	0
Walnut	9	4	0

Data derived from manufacturer's package labels.

ABOUT MAYONNAISE

Look for a product that lists a liquid vegetable oil as its first ingredient. There should be less than 2 grams of saturated fat per serving and a P:S ratio or 2:1 or higher.

COMPARISON CHART: MAYONAISSE TYPE SALAD DRESSINGS

	poly	sat	chol	per tablespoon calories
Hellmann's Chol. Free	2	1	0	50
Hellmann's Light	2	1	5	50
Hellmann's Real	5	2	5	100
Miracle Whip Chol. Free	4	1	0	70
Miracle Whip Light	2	1	0	45
Miracle Whip Real	4	1	5	70

Data derived from manufacturer's package labels.

ABOUT CHEESE

One ounce of low fat cheese is a suggested substitute for one ounce of meat. Read the labels for fat content. 5-6 grams per ounce is considered fat sparing. Look for cheeses that are part skim milk. Recommended cheeses include: part skim milk mozzarella, Alpine Lace, Jarlsburg Lite. A small amount of assertively flavored cheese such as Parmesan, delivers a lot of punch! Be aware that part skim milk cheeses are not necessarily lowfat products, but rather reduced fat. Eat sparingly!

ABOUT HEALTHY CRACKERS

There are many crackers on your grocers' shelves which are healthy as well as tasty. The following are generally good choices as they are usually low in total fat and are baked with acceptable fats and oils:

Bagel thins	Rice cakes
Bread sticks (wthout cheese)	Rye crisp
Lahvosh bread	Saltines (some are low
Matzos	sodium)
Oyster crackers	Scandinavian crisps,
Pretzels (watch for sodium)	flatbreads and hardtack

SPOTLIGHT *shows the way to healthful crackers on your grocer's shelves. Many nationally known brands have adjusted their recipes, eliminating the animal fats, palm and coconut oils and hydrogenated vegetable oils considered by the nutritional community to be unhealthy. Read labels for the cholesterol content and the type of fat. Polly wants a cracker, but nowadays, she wants it to be polyunsaturated.*

ABOUT HEALTHY SNACKS

Avoid snacks made with palm oil, cocount oil, hydrogenated vegetable oils and animal fats. Be aware that many snack foods are high in sodium. There are nuts, crackers, potato chips, pretzels, corn chips and other snack items now available unsalted and containing healthy oils. Read the labels carefully and learn to identify the healthier products.

ABOUT GROUND BEEF AND GROUND POULTRY

Many **BEGINNING LIGHT** hors d'oeuvres recipes use ground poultry as a main ingredient, often substituting chicken and turkey for the higher cholesterol beef. Our taste testers all agree that taste integrity has been maintained when this substitution has been made. Note the difference in fat content between chicken, turkey and beef.

COMPARISON CHART GROUND POULTRY AND BEEF

	Lean Beef	Extra Lean Beef	Chicken Breast	Turkey (90% fat free)
g fat	83.8	74.2	5.6	39.9
g mono	36.5	32.5	0.0	16.0
g poly	3.1	2.7	1.3	11.2
g sat	32.9	29.0	1.5	12.8
mg chol	394.9	378.9	263.1	335.4
g carb	0.0	0.0	0.0	0.0
g fiber	0.0	0.0	0.0	0.0
g protein	112.0	115.3	104.8	78.3
mg sodium	346.9	314.9	294.8	383.3
g sugar	0.0	0.0	0.0	0.0
kc calories	1233.0	1158.0	499.0	670.8

Nutritive values calculated for 1 pound (453.6 grams)

ABOUT CRAB AND MOCK CRAB

We often include canned or fresh crabmeat in our **BEGINNING LIGHT** recipes. We heartily suggest the substitution of mock crab since it is much less costly and is readily availible (but never as tasty as the "real thing"). Note that mock crab is much lower in cholesterol than canned or fresh crab, but the sodium content is considerably higher.

COMPARISON CHART: CANNED CRAB MEAT / MOCK CRAB MEAT

	Canned Crab Meat	Mock Crab Meat
g fat	10.8	5.9
g mono	2.0	0.0
g poly	6.7	0.0
g sat	2.0	0.0
mg chol	454.0	90.7
g carb	3.4	46.3
g fiber	0.0	0.0
g protein	80.6	54.4
mg sodium	2268.0	3816.0
g sugar	0.0	0.0
kc calories	454.0	464.0

Nutritive values calculated for 1 pound.

ABOUT LOWERING SODIUM CONSUMPTION

Reduce your salt intake gradually. At first, leave out half of the salt in a recipe. Later you may omit even more. Your palate will soon become accustomed to much less salt. You will find that salt is more effective when added to the surface of cooked food.

Substitute herbs, lemon juice and other assertively flavored ingredients.

To desalt soups, boil peeled potatoes in salty soup until slightly softened but not disintegrated. Remove and the excess salt will have been absorbed. A hot potato handles the salt problem!

Products labeled "cooking wine" are notoriously high in sodium. Instead, buy an inexpensive table wine for cooking purposes.

SPOTLIGHT changes its grain to salt substitutes which should be added to your food at the table. Potassium salts have an unpleasant taste if cooked. Use them sparingly, with the approval of a physician.

LOW SODIUM LEMON PEPPER

2 tablespoons cracked black pepper

1 tablespoon sour salt (citric acid)

1 tablespoon salt substitute

2 teaspoons grated lemon peel

1/8 teaspoon garlic powder

1/4 teaspoon onion powder

Combine all the ingredients.

Store in refrigerator in airtight container.

YIELD: 12 teaspooons (¼ cup)			
Nutritive Values (per teaspoon)		calories	2.7 kc
total fat	trace	carbohydrates	0.8 g
monosaturated fat	trace	fiber	0.3 g
polyunsaturated fat	trace	protein	0.1 g
saturated fat	trace	sodium	0.5 mg
cholesterol	0.0 mg	sugar	0.0 g

BEGINNING LIGHT advises heavy salters that taste for salt is a habit which can be retrained. Add salt at the table. A small amount of salt on the surface of food delivers an immediate surge of taste and minimizes its use during food preparation.

COMPARISON CHART FOR FREQUENTLY USED CANNED FOODS

Item	Quantity	Mg. Sodium
Cream Style Corn	1 cup	730.0
Cream Style Corn, low sodium	1 cup	7.7
Mustard	1 teaspoon	68.1
Mustard, low sodium	1 teaspoon	1.0
Tomato Paste	1 cup	2070.0
Tomato Paste, low sodium	1 cup	172.0
Catsup	1 tablespoon	156.0
Catsup, low sodium	1 tablespoon	110.0
Dill Pickle	1 medium	1856.0
Spaghetti Sauce	1 cup	1236.0
Fresh Tomato Pizza Sauce (Page 239)	1 cup	309.3
Tomato Sauce	1 cup	1481.0
Tomato Sauce, low sodium	1 cup	65.0
Tomatoes, Canned	1 cup	390.0
Tomatoes, Canned, low sodium	1 cup	31.2
Tomato Juice	1 cup	882.0
Tomato Juice, low sodium	1 cup	24.4

SPOTLIGHT *suggests rinsing high sodium foodstuffs such as processed foods, canned vegetables and cottage cheese. Also, soaking the following in cold water for fifteen minutes, changing water once or twice: anchovies, capers, feta cheese, ham bones and pickled vegetables.*

MUST WE AVOID EGGS?

BEGINNING LIGHT urges that you don't arbitrarily eliminate eggs from your recipes because of their cholesterol content. In recipes calling for several eggs, discard half of the egg yolks. You may replace the fat content with 1-2 teaspoons of a recomended vegetable oil.

MAKE YOUR OWN EGG SUBSTITUTE

1 egg white	2 teaspoons powdered skim milk
2 teaspoons vegetable oil	Yellow food coloring (optional)

These ingredients can either be combined or added to recipe without premixing. (Add skim milk powder with dry ingredients and remaining ingredients with liquids).

EGG COMPARISON CHART

	Fresh Raw Egg	Make Your Own Egg Substitute
g fat	5.0	4.5
g mono	1.9	3.3
g poly	0.6	0.4
g fsat	1.5	0.7
mg chol	213.0	0.2
g carb	0.6	0.9
g fiber	0.0	0.0
g protein	6.2	3.9
mg sodium	63.0	60.4
g sugar	0.0	0.5
kc calories	80.0	60.0

Nutritive values calculated for 1 large egg or equivalent.

There are several commercial egg substitute products availible in markets. They have a varying fat content.

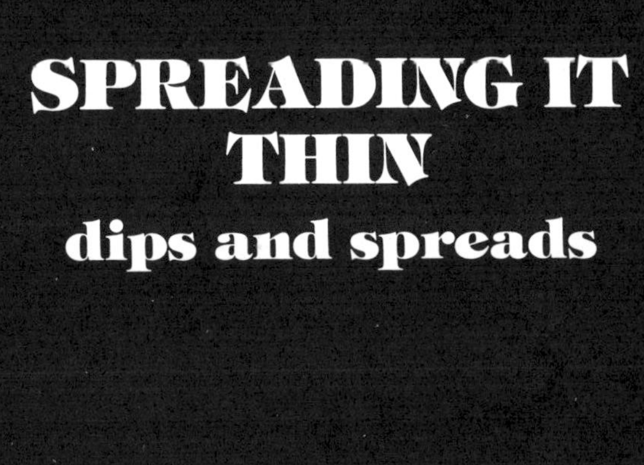

7

SPREADING IT
THIN
dips and spreads

♥ WHITE CHILI STRATA

Your food processor will be your "best friend" as you make this quick and easy wow of an hors d'oeuvre.

2	15-ounce cans Northern Beans (white), drained
2	cloves garlic, peeled
1	teaspoon vegetable oil
1/2	pound boneless, skinless chicken breast, ground (may be ground in food processor using steel blade)
1/4-1/2	teaspoon mild or hot chili powder
1	cup chopped onion
1	8-ounce can mild or hot green chilies, chopped
1	8-ounce jar mild or hot salsa
8	ounces fat reduced cheddar, colby or Monterey Jack cheese, grated

1. Using steel blade, process beans and garlic until smooth. Spoon in even layer into 9x11 inch oven-proof serving dish with 1½ inch to 2 inch sides. Set aside.

2. Brown ground chicken breast in oil, breaking the chicken into small pieces as it cooks. Mix in chili powder.

3. Cover bean layer with cooked ground chicken.

4. Add layer of chopped onion, chilies, then salsa.

5. Cover dish loosely with foil. Bake in preheated 350° oven for 25-30 minutes.

6. Sprinkle with cheese. Return to oven 2-3 minutes or until cheese is melted.

7. Remove from oven. Cool 5 minutes before serving with acceptable crackers or chips (Page 138).

YIELD: 5 cups

Nutritive Values (per tablespoon)		calories	22.7 kc
total fat	0.5 g	carbohydrates	3.0 g
monosaturated fat	0.1 g	fiber	0.6 g
polyunsaturated fat	0.0 g	protein	1.3 g
saturated fat	0.2 g	sodium	31.6 mg
cholesterol	2.5 mg	sugar	0.1 g

TACO PIE

This tastes as good as it looks!

*2 cups low fat yogurt, drained 4 hours
1 tablespoon lemon juice
1 small ripe avocado, mashed
¾ teaspoon chili powder
1 teaspoon garlic salt
   Pepper to taste

2 tablespoons chopped onion
   Shredded lettuce
1 large tomato, chopped
1 cup shredded low fat cheddar or low fat colby cheese
¼ cup baco bits
   Taco sauce

1. Combine first 6 ingredients in a blender or food processor; blend well.

2. Pour mixture onto a serving dish (such as a large glass pizza dish). Top with onion, lettuce, tomato, cheese and baco bits. Sprinkle with taco sauce.

For flavors to blend, refrigerate for at least 2 hours before serving. Serve with crackers.

*ALL ABOUT YOGURT (Page 154)

While avocado is high in fat content and calories this unsaturated fat is healthy when consumed in small amounts. ASPARAGUS GUACAMOLE (Page 153) may be substituted for the first 6 ingredients for lower fat content (omit tomato).

YIELD: 8 servings

Nutritive Values (per serving)		calories	139.5 kc
total fat	8.3 g	carbohydrates	9.1 g
monosaturated fat	3.3 g	fiber	1.5 g
polyunsaturated fat	2.0 g	protein	9.6 g
saturated fat	1.5 g	sodium	391.9 mg
cholesterol	3.5 mg	sugar	3.7 g

GREAT GARBANZO DIP

Garbanzo beans contain generous amounts of water soluble fiber, so effective in reducing cholesterol.

2 cloves garlic, finely chopped	* ¾ cup plain low fat yogurt, drained 1 hour
1 tablespoon olive oil	¼ teaspoon freshly ground pepper
2½ cups cooked garbanzo beans, drained	½ teaspoon paprika
4 teaspoons fresh lemon juice	Salt to taste
1 teaspoon ground cumin	

1. Sauté garlic in olive oil for 2 minutes.

2. Using steel knife, chop garbanzo beans with lemon juice in food processor until smooth.

3. Add remaining ingredients; process ½ minute. Add salt to taste.

Serve with vegetables, TORTILLA CRAX (Page 255), or PITA TRIANGLES (Page 255) for dipping.

For a spicier flavor, stir in:
 ¼ cup chopped onion
 1 tablespoon diced jalapeño peppers
 ¼ cup each diced red and yellow peppers

*ALL ABOUT YOGURT (Page 154)

To reduce sodium content rinse garbanzo beans in cold water and use salt substitute.

YIELD: 3 cups

Nutritive Values (per tablespoon)		calories	16.7 kc
total fat	2.3 g	carbohydrates	2.3 g
monosaturated fat	0.2 g	fiber	0.6 g
polyunsaturated fat	trace	protein	0.8 g
saturated fat	trace	sodium	58.5 mg
cholesterol	0.2 mg	sugar	0.2 g

RED BEAN PIE

1	29-ounce can red kidney beans, drained
*1	cup low fat yogurt, drained 4 hours
1	4-ounce can chopped black olives
1	4-ounce can green chiles, chopped
**1	cup salsa (commercial or PLUM TOMATO SALSA (Page 240)
1	large tomato, diced and drained
2	tablespoons chopped onion
4	hard cooked egg whites, chopped
4	ounces shredded low-fat colby

1. Process beans in food processor until smooth. Spoon in thin layer on 12-14 inch platter.

2. Cover with yogurt.

3. Sprinkle evenly with remaining ingredients.

Dip with light cholesterol-free nacho chips, tortilla chips or TOASTED PITA TRIANGLES (Page 255).

*ALL ABOUT YOGURT (Page 154)

**If commercial salsa seems too watery, drain it a bit.

To reduce sodium, rinse beans and substitute low sodium salsa.

YIELD: 10 servings

Nutritive Values (per serving)		calories	142.8 kc
total fat	4.7 g	carbohydrates	19.0 g
monosaturated fat	1.9 g	fiber	4.6 g
polyunsaturated fat	0.2 g	protein	9.6 g
saturated fat	1.0 g	sodium	528.6 mg
cholesterol	5.0 mg	sugar	2.0 g

HUMMUS BI TAHINI

Chick Peas with Sesame Seed

The tahini or sesame paste can be purchased in any Greek food store. The paste is made from sesame meal. This recipe is most widely known and appreciated in the Middle East.

1	pound can chick peas	1	cup tahini (sesame seed paste)
	Juice of 4-6 lemons, to taste		Paprika
4-6	cloves garlic, crushed	2	tablespoons finely chopped parsley
1	teaspoon salt		

1. Drain chick peas. Put aside 10 for garnish.

2. In food processor, pour in lemon juice and a few drops of water. Add tahini, garlic and salt. Process, adding chick peas, a few at a time, until it reaches the consistency of a creamy paste. If paste remains too thick, add water or lemon juice, a little at a time. Adjust seasoning (lemon, garlic, salt).

Garnish with paprika, parsley and reserved chick peas.

Serve with PITA TRIANGLES (Page 255) for dipping.

SPOTLIGHT *suggests that HUMMUS makes a delectable filling for hard boiled egg boats. Save cholesterol, add fiber and don't end up with egg on your face.*

To reduce sodium use salt substitute and rinse the chick peas.

YIELD: 12 servings

Nutritive Values (per serving)		calories	154.0 kc
total fat	10.0 g	carbohydrates	13.4 g
monosaturated fat	3.5 g	fiber	5.0 g
polyunsaturated fat	4.1 g	protein	5.5 g
saturated fat	1.3 g	sodium	331.0 mg
cholesterol	0.0 mg	sugar	0.8 g

CAPONATA

1 eggplant (1 pound)
1 cup chopped onion
1-2 cloves garlic
½ cup chopped green
   pepper
2 tablespoons olive oil
2 tablespoons lemon
   juice
*1 tablespoon toasted
   sesame seed
2 tablespoons chopped
   parsley
**1 cup peeled, finely
   diced and drained
   plum tomatoes

2 teaspoons sugar
1½ teaspoons chopped
   basil (½ teaspoon
   dried)
1½ teaspoons chopped
   oregano
   (½ teaspoon dried)
   Freshly ground pepper
2-4 teaspoons chopped
   fresh ginger
   (optional)
¼ teaspoon red pepper
   flakes (optional)
3 tablespoons capers

1. Cook eggplant in covered pot in 2 inches of water until
   soft when pierced with a fork.
   or
   Prick eggplant ten times with fork. Place in pan and
   bake at 400° for 1 hour or until soft.
   or
   Place on 3 layers of paper toweling, prick with fork and
   microwave at full power for 12-15 minutes or until tender,
   rotating every 3 minutes.

2. While eggplant is baking, sauté onion, green pepper and
   garlic in olive oil for 5 minutes.

3. Peel eggplant and discard skin. Process eggplant and
   sautéed vegetables in food processor with steel blade,
   with several on-off pulses, until coarsely chopped.

CAPONATA *(continued)*

4. Stir in remaining ingredients, adding freshly ground pepper to taste.

5. Garnish with capers.

Serve hot or cold with pita bread, crackers, party rye, or Italian bread.

Store 1 week in refrigerator or freeze.

**SPOTLIGHT (Page 203)

***SPOTLIGHT** on toasting nuts and sesame seeds: place them in a dry skillet over a medium-high heat. Cook until lightly browned, stirring frequently to prevent burning.*

YIELD: 4 cups

Nutritive Values (per tablespoon)		calories	10.0 kc
total fat	0.6 g	carbohydrates	1.3 g
monosaturated fat	0.4 g	fiber	0.4 g
polyunsaturated fat	0.1 g	protein	0.2 g
saturated fat	0.1 g	sodium	11.6 mg
cholesterol	0.0 mg	sugar	0.5 g

MUSTARD MADNESS

1	16-ounce package frozen chopped mustard greens	2	tablespoons diced pimiento
*3	cups low fat yogurt, drained 4 hours	1	tablespoon chopped green onions
½	cup lite mayonnaise	2	tablespoons fresh dill weed (2 teaspoons dried)
½	tablespoon olive oil		
2	teaspoons mustard seed	¼	teaspoon salt
			Few grinds pepper
½	cup coarsely chopped water chestnuts	6	drops Tabasco

Thaw frozen mustard greens; squeeze out as much excess liquid as possible. Combine with remaining ingredients; refrigerate for at least 4 hours or overnight to allow flavors to blend.

Use MUSTARD MADNESS as a spread—or as a filler for:
    Celery stalks (Page 80)
    Endive stalks (Page 80)
    EGG BOATS (Page 116)
    Cherry tomatoes (Page 81)
    Mushroom caps (Page 81)

It may also be used as a dip for crisp vegetables.

*ALL ABOUT YOGURT (Page 154)

YIELD: 4½ cups

Nutritive Values (per tablespoon)		calories	11.4 kc
total fat	0.5 g	carbohydrates	1.1 g
monosaturated fat	0.1 g	fiber	0.1 g
polyunsaturated fat	0.0 g	protein	0.7 g
saturated fat	0.0 g	sodium	14.2 mg
cholesterol	0.7 mg	sugar	0.4 g

ASPARAGUS GUACAMOLE

1 pound fresh or frozen asparagus spears steamed until tender

1 tablespoon lemon juice

3 tablespoons chopped sweet onion

*1 large tomato, peeled

¼ teaspoon chili powder

1 small clove garlic

Dash Tabasco

**¼ cup low fat yogurt, drained 5 minutes on paper towel

1 teaspoon lemon pepper

Place all ingredients in food processor with steel blade. Process until smooth. Pour into serving bowl.

Serve with cherry tomatoes, tortilla chips.

*SPOTLIGHT (Page 203)

**ALL ABOUT YOGURT (Page 154)

YIELD: 2 cups			
Nutritive Values (per tablespoon)		calories	6.0 kc
total fat	0.1 g	carbohydrates	1.1 g
monosaturated fat	0.0 g	fiber	0.2 g
polyunsaturated fat	0.0 g	protein	0.5 g
saturated fat	0.0 g	sodium	35.8 mg
cholesterol	0.1 mg	sugar	0.4 g

ALL ABOUT YOGURT

2,500 years ago yogurt was called "food for the Gods" because of its positive effect upon those fortunate citizens who consumed it. Of Turkish origin, yogurt is recognized today as being far more easily digested than milk, and far more acceptable to those whose everyday diet demands a low fat, low calorie dairy product.

Yogurt is an extremely healthy ingredient for use in hors d'oeuvre recipes which use sour cream (low fat yogurt has 140 calories per cup; sour cream, 445 calories per cup), cream cheese (790 calories per cup) or mayonnaise (1,585 calories per cup).

One may produce a dairy product which is of dip or spread consistency by simply draining excess liquid whey from yogurt which contains no gelatin or stablizer. Dannon™ Yogurt is an example of commercial yogurt which meets this specification.

EQUIPMENT

1. A drainer made specifically for this purpose may be purchased in your supermarket or in a health food store.
2. It is possible to make your own yogurt drainer by placing 2 or 3 pieces of paper towel in a strainer supported by the sides of a bowl or glass into which it is draining. Place fresh yogurt in this strainer and refrigerate for 2-4 hours, depending upon the consistency of "cheese" desired.
3. Drain off excess whey by filling the filter-lined top of your drip coffee maker with yogurt and catching the liquid in the base.

DRAINING YOGURT

The following results were recorded in our kitchens hourly to document the amount of liquid drained from 3 cups of yogurt:

Number of Hours	1	2	3	4	5	14	20
Total ounces of drainage	6	8	9	9½	11	12¼	12¾

Approximately 1½ cups remains after 24 hours.

Notice that the greatest amount of draining occurs within the first few hours. Very little whey will drain out after 24 hours. Further absorption is possible however: spread the drained yogurt on 3 or 4 layers of paper towel and wrap it up for just a few minutes. The towel will peel away from the resulting "cheese."

CHUTNEY CHEESE PÂTÉ

This interesting blend of flavors works well with either reduced fat cheddar or tofu cheddar.

*1¼ cups low fat yogurt, drained 24 hours
4 ounces tofu cheddar or reduced fat cheddar, shredded
2 tablespoons dry sherry

½ teaspoon curry powder
¼ teaspoon salt
¾ cup chutney or MANGO CHUTNEY (Page 237)
2 whole green onions, finely chopped

1. Mix first 5 ingredients thoroughly. Spread in 6 inch circle on pie plate; chill.

2. Spread chutney over cheese and top with green onions.

Serve with some interesting crackers or party rye.

*ALL ABOUT YOGURT (Page 154)

SPOTLIGHT *on tofu cheese; use tofu cheese to replace milk base cheeses in your favorite recipes. They are quite adaptable. Mozzarella worked well with PIZZA (Page 223) and cheddar was a viable option in cheese balls and PITA (Page 227) and TORTILLA PIZZAS (Page 228).*

Nutritive analysis computed with reduced fat cheddar.

YIELD: 8 servings			
Nutritive Values (per serving)		calories	142.1 kc
total fat	4.1 g	carbohydrates	25.1 g
monosaturated fat	0.6 g	fiber	trace g
polyunsaturated fat	17.9 g	protein	53.0 g
saturated fat	2.5 g	sodium	247.0 mg
cholesterol	109.5 mg	sugar	16.7 g

MOCK BOURSIN au POIVRE

This versatile spread tastes like the costly French Boursin au Poivre. It is always a great hit. We use it as an ingredient in several of our recipes.

*1	pint low fat yogurt, drained 24 hours	1	teaspoon dried dill weed
1	clove garlic, crushed	1	teaspoon chopped chives, dehydrated
1	teaspoon caraway seed		Lemon pepper
1	teaspoon dried basil		

1. Blend drained yogurt with next 5 ingredients.

2. Pat into round flat shape. wrap tightly in plastic film and refrigerate.

3. Roll generously on all sides in lemon pepper.

Make a day in advance to permit flavors to blend.

*ALL ABOUT YOGURT (Page 154)

SPOTLIGHT *is on double savings with MOCK BOURSIN AU POIVRE. Made with drained low fat yogurt, the careful cook saves both calories and cash by switching from the expensive high fat cheese to a low fat alternative. Show your care and earn your interest—good health!*

To reduce sodium, substitute LOW SODIUM LEMON PEPPER (Page 140)

YIELD: 1 cup

Nutritive Values (per tablespoon)		calories	20.0 kc
total fat	0.5 g	carbohydrates	2.4 g
monosaturated fat	0.1 g	fiber	trace
polyunsaturated fat	trace	protein	1.6 g
saturated fat	0.3 g	sodium	286.0 mg
cholesterol	1.8 mg	sugar	1.5 g

SUN DRIED TOMATOES WITH MOCK BOURSIN

An elegant hors d'oeuvre presentation

1. Make a 4-6 inch mold of MOCK BOURSIN (Page 156).

2. Surround with a row of reconstituted sun dried tomatoes that have been marinated in garlic flavored olive oil. Encircle with party rye slices.

TO RECONSTITUTE SUN DRIED TOMATOES:

Microwave:

Place of sun dried tomatoes in oven proof dish. Cover with water, then loosely cover with plastic wrap. Microwave on HIGH until water boils (1-2 minutes). Allow tomatoes to steep in covered water for 5 more minutes until soft. Drain thoroughly on paper towel.

Stovetop:

Place in pan of boiling water; cover. Remove from stove and steep for 10 minutes.

TO MARINATE SUN DRIED TOMATOES:

Place reconstituted tomatoes in sufficient olive oil to coat. Add one minced garlic clove. Refrigerate for at least 4 hours before serving and drain well on paper towels. May be stored in refrigerator for future use.

VARIATION:

Alternate slices of lox (smoked salmon) with sundried tomatoes.

MIX 'n MATCH DIP BASES AND SPREADS

Why use high fat, high cholesterol sour cream and cream cheese in your dips and spreads? Here are some healthy alternatives which will fool your eye and your palate, yet satisfy your taste buds. Try them all!

These recipes are dip and spread bases. They simulate the high fat, high cholesterol sour cream and cream cheese products, yet retain a rich dairy flavor. They are interchangeable and are meant as a tasty base for your favorite ingredients into a delicious dish.

COMPARATIVE NUTRIENT VALUES FOR DIP BASES

Nutrient Values (per tablespoon)	COTTAGE CHEESE DIP BASE	RICOTTA YOGURT DIP BASE	COTTAGE CHEESE YOGURT DIP BASE	TOFU DIP BASE	MOCK SOUR CREAM DIP BASE
g total fat	trace	trace	0.3	2.9	0.1
g monosaturated fat	trace	trace	trace	1.5	trace
g polyunsaturated fat	trace	trace	trace	0.8	trace
g saturated fat	trace	trace	0.2	0.4	trace
g cholesterol	0.6	0.7	1.1	0.0	0.6
kc calories	9.0	7.0	6.0	36.0	10.0
g carbohydrates	0.5	0.4	0.4	0.7	0.6
g fiber	0.0	trace	0.0	0.2	trace
g protein	1.5	1.3	0.6	2.2	1.6
mg sodium	47.0	202.0	6.7	1.9	94.0
g sugar	0.4	trace	0.2	trace	0.4

YOGURT MOCK CREAM CHEESE

To make 1 cup of yogurt cream cheese, drain 2 cups of low fat yogurt for 24 hours. For further drying, place drained yogurt between layers of paper towels for 5 minutes, patting to dry.

MIX AND MATCH DIP BASES

COTTAGE CHEESE DIP BASE

1   cup low fat cottage cheese
1¼ cups skim milk

Process in food processor, using steel blade, until well blended.

COTTAGE CHEESE YOGURT DIP BASE

2   cups dry cottage cheese
½   cup non fat yogurt - don't drain

Process in food processor, using steel blade, until well blended.

RICOTTA YOGURT DIP BASE

½   cup plain non fat yogurt
½   cup ricotta

Process in food processor, using steel blade, until well blended.

MOCK SOUR CREAM DIP BASE

1½ cups low fat cottage cheese
1   tablespoon fresh lemon juice
1-2 tablespoons low fat buttermilk
1½ teaspoons salt
Few grains of pepper

1. Place cottage cheese in strainer: rinse under cold running water. Drain remaining liquid on paper towels.
2. Blend above ingredients in food processor, using steel blade, until smooth. (Add only enough buttermilk to obtain desired consistency.) If other flavorings are liquid, delay adding buttermilk until all other liquids are incorporated.

To reduce sodium, use salt substitute.

TOFU DIP BASE

½   pound tofu, drained
1   tablespoon fresh lemon juice
2   tablespoons vegetable oil

Blend in food processor, using steel blade, until smooth and thick.

VEGETABLE DIP

A crunchy, munchy delight!

1 cup DIP BASE of your choice (Page 159)
1 tablespoon chopped carrot
2 tablespoons chopped water chestnuts
2 teaspoons chopped onion

1 teaspoon each chopped green and red pepper
½ teaspoon salt or salt substitute
⅛ teaspoon garlic salt or pinch of garlic powder
Dash white pepper

1. Combine all ingredients.

2. Cover and chill.

Serve with raw vegetables (CRUDITÉS, Page 161) and crackers.

Dip Base not included in nutritive analysis. Nutritive values for Dip Bases are on page 158.

YIELD: 1 cup

Nutritive Values (per tablespoon)		calories	0.7 kc
total fat	trace	carbohydrates	0.2 g
monosaturated fat	trace	fiber	trace
polyunsaturated fat	trace	protein	trace
saturated fat	trace	sodium	86.0 mg
cholesterol	trace	sugar	trace

CRUDITÉS

A colorful arrangement of veggies

Asparagus tips	**Kohlrabi chunks**
Radishes	**Cauliflower flowerets**
Celery sticks	**Broccoli flowerets**
Carrot sticks	**Turnip slices**
Mushrooms	**Jicama strips**
Pea pods	**Black olives**
Cucumber slices	**Zucchini or summer**
Cherry tomatoes	**squash slices**

To serve, arrange vegetables attractively (to display the different colors) on a tray, in a basket, in a cheese crate, or in a large glass bowl. Garnish with kale leaves, parsley, or watercress.

Note: Crudité means "raw" in French. Quick *blanching not only makes the vegetables look better, but also keeps them fresh longer. They can be prepared 1 or 2 days in advance, and kept refrigerated in plastic bags.

*SPOTLIGHT (Page 77)

CURRY DIP WITH CRUDITÉS

1	recipe TOFU DIP BASE (Page 159)	⅓	cup MANGO CHUTNEY (Page 237)
1	teaspoon curry powder	¼	teaspoon cumin
			Cayenne to taste

Combine all ingredients. Refrigerate, covered.

YIELD: 1 cup

Nutritive Values (per tablespoon)		calories	224.1 kc
total fat	3.8 g	carbohydrates	51.2 g
monosaturated fat	0.9 g	fiber	2.0 g
polyunsaturated fat	1.8 g	protein	3.4 g
saturated fat	0.5 g	sodium	145.3 mg
cholesterol	0.0 mg	sugar	39.1 g

SIESTA MEXICAN DIP

Let the fiesta begin. Olé!

*1   pint low fat yogurt, drained 2 hours
1-3 tablespoons chopped green chili peppers (canned)
2-4 tablespoons mild salsa or taco sauce

Mix together and chill until ready to use.

Serve with raw vegetables or chips.

For a spicier dip, use hot salsa.

*ALL ABOUT YOGURT (Page 154)

SPOTLIGHT *goes south of the border with salsa, a flavorful condiment. Be aware that some commercial salsas may be high in sodium. Try BEGINNING LIGHT'S own PLUM TOMATO SALSA (Page 240) and you'll say "si, si" without saying "salt, salt."*

YIELD: 1½ cups

Nutritive Values (per tablespoon)		calories		13.0 kc
total fat	0.3 g	carbohydrates		1.5 g
monosaturated fat	0.1 g	fiber		0.0 g
polyunsaturated fat	trace	protein		1.0 g
saturated fat	0.2 g	sodium		20.0 mg
cholesterol	1.1 mg	sugar		1 g

CARAWAY DIP

Low calorie

1	teaspoon caraway seeds	¼	teaspoon basil leaves, crushed
1	tablespoon chopped green onion		Salt and pepper to taste
*1⅓	cups low fat yogurt, drained 4 hours		

1. Combine all ingredients.

2. Add salt and pepper to taste.

3. Chill several hours.

Serve with raw vegetables, CRUDITÉS (Page 161).

*ALL ABOUT YOGURT (Page 154).

YIELD: 1 cup

Nutritive Values (per tablespoon)		calories	12.7 kc
total fat	0.3 g	carbohydrates	1.5 g
monosaturated fat	trace	fiber	trace
polyunsaturated fat	trace	protein	1.0 g
saturated fat	0.2 g	sodium	13.2 mg
cholesterol	1.1 mg	sugar	1.0 g

GARDEN DELIGHT

A particularly tasty dip when made with fresh herbs.

16 ounces dry cottage cheese
⅓ cup nonfat yogurt
1 tablespoon fresh basil (1 teaspoon dried)
½ teaspoon fresh thyme (3 pinches dried)
1 tablespoon marjoram (1 teaspoon dried)
1 teaspoon grated onion
2 tablespoons chopped celery leaves
A few drops Tabasco

1. Process all ingredients in food processor using steel blade. Add more yogurt if necessary for desired consistency for either spread or dip.

2. Refrigerate overnight to blend flavors.

Serve with raw vegetables, CRUDITÉS (Page 161).

SPOTLIGHT *suggests the ratio of 1:3 when substituting dry herbs for fresh.. When Herb isn't fresh, you need less of him!*

YIELD: 2 cups

Nutritive Values (per tablespoon)		calories	14.0 kc
total fat	trace	carbohydrates	0.6 g
monosaturated fat	trace	fiber	trace
polyunsaturated fat	trace	protein	2.6 g
saturated fat	trace	sodium	4.9 mg
cholesterol	1.0 mg	sugar	0.2 g

ARTICHOKE SMOOTHY

1 6½-ounce jar marinated artichoke hearts
*1 cup low fat yogurt, drained 4 hours

1 teaspoon Parmesan
½ teaspoon onion salt
3 drops Tabasco
2 teaspoons capers (garnish)

1. Place artichokes with liquid in food processor. Use steel blade. Blend, scraping down sides as needed until completely smooth.

2. Add remaining ingredients; blend ½ minute.

3. Refrigerate at least 1 hour. Garnish with capers.

Serve with CRUDITÉS (Page 161) and crackers for dipping.

*ALL ABOUT YOGURT (Page 154)

YIELD: 1½ cups

Nutritive Values (per tablespoon)		calories	14.0 kc
total fat	0.8 g	carbohydrates	1.0 g
monosaturated fat	0.2 g	fiber	0.0 g
polyunsaturated fat	0.3 g	protein	0.8 g
saturated fat	0.2 g	sodium	68.4 mg
cholesterol	0.7 mg	sugar	0.5 g

CLAM DIP

1 7½-ounce can minced clams	1 tablespoon lemon juice
1½ cups DIP BASE of your choice (Page 159)	½ teaspoon grated onion ½ teaspoon lemon pepper

1. Drain clams, reserving juice.

2. Blend in next three ingredients and enough clam juice to obtain desired consistency. Add salt and pepper to taste.

Serve with vegetables for dipping, CRUDITÉS (Page 161).

Nutritive values calculated with commercial lemon pepper. Use LOW SODIUM LEMON PEPPER (Page 140) to reduce sodium. The nutritive content of dip base is not included.

YIELD: 2 cups

Nutritive Values (per tablespoon)		calories	3.0 kc
total fat	trace	carbohydrates	0.2 g
monosaturated fat	trace	fiber	trace
polyunsaturated fat	trace	protein	0.5 g
saturated fat	trace	sodium	20.1 mg
cholesterol	4.1 mg	sugar	trace g

GEFILTE FISH DIP

Extremely low calorie taste treat!

***1** pound jar gefilte fish in jellied liquid broth

1 teaspoon lemon juice

2 teaspoons prepared white horseradish

Dash pepper

1. Drain fish, reserving broth.

2. Blend fish in food processor with 3 tablespoons reserved broth and remaining ingredients.

3. Refrigerate for about 1 hour.

Serve with party rye or caraway wafers.

*Try our quick and easy food processor method of making your own GEFILTE FISH (Page 110).

YIELD: 1½ cups

Nutritive Values (per tablespoon)		calories	16.0 kc
total fat	0.3 g	carbohydrates	1.5 g
monosaturated fat	0.2 g	fiber	trace
polyunsaturated fat	trace	protein	1.7 g
saturated fat	0.1 g	sodium	105.0 mg
cholesterol	5.4 mg	sugar	trace

HERRING SPREAD

Delicious! It will become an old stand-by in your hors d'oeuvres repertoire. You'll love the crunch of the mustard seed.

1	12-ounce jar herring in wine sauce	*1	pint low fat yogurt, drained 4 hours
2	tablespoons dehydrated onion	2	teaspoons mustard seed
2	teaspoons sugar	½	cup chopped tart apple

1. Drain herring on paper towels.

2. Chop herring and mix with remaining ingredients.

Make a day ahead. Serve with party rye.

*ALL ABOUT YOGURT (Page 154)

To reduce sodium, rinse herring with cold water and drain on paper towels.

YIELD: 2 cups

Nutritive Values (per tablespoon)		calories	40.0 kc
total fat	2.2 g	carbohydrates	3.6 g
monosaturated fat	1.4 g	fiber	trace
polyunsaturated fat	0.2 g	protein	2.6 g
saturated fat	0.4 g	sodium	102.0 mg
cholesterol	2.2 mg	sugar	1.2 g

TUNA WHIP

1   6½-ounce can white
    meat tuna packed in
    water, drained
1   cup low fat cottage
    cheese

1-2 tablespoons lite
    mayonnaise
1-2 tablespoons grated
    onion
1   tablespoon low calorie
    Italian dressing

Blend in food processor.

Serve with vegetables, crackers or toasted
PITA TRIANGLES (Page 255).

To reduce sodium, use salt free tuna fish and salt substitute.

YIELD: 2 cups

Nutritive Values (per tablespoon)		calories	16.0 kc
total fat	0.5 g	carbohydrates	0.3 g
monosaturated fat	0.1 g	fiber	trace
polyunsaturated fat	0.2 g	protein	2.4 g
saturated fat	0.1 g	sodium	56.0 mg
cholesterol	2.7 mg	sugar	0.2 g

SHERRIED MUSHROOM PÂTÉ

A Crowd Pleaser

½ cup onion, finely chopped
2 tablespoons margarine
2 tablespoons sherry
½ teaspoon seasoned salt
8 ounces fresh mushrooms, finely chopped
1 tablespoon lemon juice
1 teaspoon Worcestershire sauce
2 tablespoons lite Hellmann's or Best Foods mayonnaise
Pepper
Dill weed for garnish

1. Sauté onion in margarine until golden.

2. Add mushrooms, seasoned salt and sherry. Continue cooking until liquid is absorbed.

3. Add lemon juice and Worcestershire sauce. Remove from heat.

4. Add mayonnaise and freshly ground pepper to taste. Garnish with dill weed.

5. Refrigerate for at least 4 hours.

Serve with crackers.

This also can be served on lettuce as a salad.

YIELD: 6 servings

Nutritive Values (per serving)		calories	78.0 kc
total fat	6.2 g	carbohydrates	4.2 g
monosaturated fat	1.6 g	fiber	0.7 g
polyunsaturated fat	2.5 g	protein	9.8 g
saturated fat	0.8 g	sodium	254.6 mg
cholesterol	0.0 mg	sugar	1.1 g

WATERCRESS ROLLUPS

*1¾ cups low fat yogurt,
   drained 24 hours
1 teaspoon minced
   onion
1 small clove garlic
1 bunch watercress
1 tablespoon prepared
   horseradish

½ teaspoon salt
¼ teaspoon pepper
1 teaspoon
   Worcestershire
8 slices fresh bread,
   crusts removed

1. Blend all ingredients except bread in food processor until smooth.

2. Flatten bread with rolling pin.

3. Spread watercress mixture on bread slices. Refrigerate until firm. Roll up jelly roll fashion, then slice into bite-sized pieces.

*ALL ABOUT YOGURT (Page 154)

SPOTLIGHT *offers a low fat, low cholesterol, inexpensive version of a costly French cheese, MOCK BOURSIN AU POIVRE! It's an hors d'oeuvres lover's delight, served alone or used as a filler in several BEGINNING LIGHT recipes. "The cheese stands alone" is not always the case.*

YIELD: 32 pieces			
Nutritive Values (per piece)		calories	25.0 kc
total fat	0.4 g	carbohydrates	4.0 g
monosaturated fat	0.1 g	fiber	0.2 g
polyunsaturated fat	0.0 g	protein	1.2 g
saturated fat	0.2 g	sodium	80.9 mg
cholesterol	0.7 mg	sugar	0.9 g

PURE GARLIC SPREAD

Serve this pure garlic spread instead of butter to a group of friends who love garlic and who associate mostly with each other!

2   **whole heads elephant garlic (1 pound)**
    Olive oil spray
    Salt free herb seasoning mix
2-4 teaspoons olive oil

1. Peel outer skin from garlic heads.

2. Spray garlic cloves with oil. Dust lightly with seasoning mix.

3. Place in cooking bag. Close bag with twister. Place in pan with 1 inch sides. Make air holes in bag according to manufacturer's directions. May also be wrapped in aluminum foil.

4. Bake at 350° for 40 minutes.

5. When cooled, squeeze creamy contents of each garlic clove into bowl of food processor. Add olive oil. Using steel blade, blend until smooth. (Your mini-food processor is perfect for this recipe.)

6. Refrigerate in tightly sealed container. It is perishable.

Serve as you would butter, perhaps in a small crock. As a gourmet touch for an Italian meal, shape as a flowerette and place on individual bread and butter plates.

Serving suggestion: spread on whole wheat bread, then toast under broiler.

Nutrient values calculated with lower amount of olive oil.

YIELD: ¾ cup

Nutritive Values (per teaspoon)		calories	20.0 kc
total fat	0.5 g	carbohydrates	4.1 g
monosaturated fat	0.3 g	fiber	0.0 g
polyunsaturated fat	0.0 g	protein	0.8 g
saturated fat	0.1 g	sodium	4.2 mg
cholesterol	0.0 mg	sugar	0.1 g

8

SOUP'S ON

TURKEY BEAN SOUP

Serve with CORNY CORN MUFFINS (Page 257).

2½ cups navy beans
1 turkey leg, skin removed
3 quarts water
1½ cups coarsely chopped carrots
1¼ cups coarsely chopped potato

1¼ cups coarsely chopped onion
¼ teaspoon pepper
3-4 dashes Tabasco
   Salt or salt substitute to taste

1. Wash beans, cover with water and soak overnight. Drain water and discard. Place in large kettle with turkey leg and water.

2. Bring to a boil. Reduce heat and simmer, covered, for 1½ hours. Remove turkey leg and continue cooking until beans are tender.

3. Remove meat from turkey leg. Cool and shred. Return to soup along with remaining ingredients. Continue cooking for 30 minutes.

For a smoky taste, use smoked turkey leg.

SPOTLIGHT *on beans: beans are complex carbohydrates, high in soluble fiber and protein, low in fat and sodium and contain no cholesterol. However, they are not a "complete protein." Combined with a grain, they become complete.*

YIELD: 12 servings

Nutritive Values (per serving)		calories	117.4 kc
total fat	2.9 g	carbohydrates	10.0 g
monosaturated fat	0.6 g	fiber	0.5 g
polyunsaturated fat	0.9 g	protein	12.5 g
saturated fat	0.9 g	sodium	223.8 mg
cholesterol	32.1 mg	sugar	1.8 g

WILD RICE SOUP

A delicious soup from the wild rice country of Minnesota

1 turkey thigh or 5 chicken thighs, skin removed

9 cups chicken broth, fat removed

2 tablespoons minced onion

1 bay leaf

½ teaspoon thyme

6 peppercorns

1 large onion, cut into 8 pieces

½ green pepper, quartered

2 ribs celery with leaves, cut into 2 inch pieces

*8 ounces fresh mushrooms

¼ cup margarine

½ cup flour

1 cup wild rice, cooked until tender and drained

1 cup skim milk

Salt and pepper to taste

Chopped parsley for garnish

1. Place first 6 ingredients in soup pot. Cover and simmer for 1-2 hours or until meat is tender. (Turkey will require the 2 hours, chicken just 1 hour.)

2. Strain stock. Chill and remove solidified fat.

3. Remove meat from bones and shred; add to stock.

4. Chop onion, green pepper, celery and mushrooms in food processor using steel blade.

WILD RICE SOUP *(continued)*

5. Melt margarine in soup pot. Add chopped vegetables and
   sauté until tender-crisp. Stir in flour and cook for
   4 minutes, stirring frequently. Gradually stir in stock.
   Cook over medium heat until lightly thickened, stirring
   frequently. Stir in cooked rice and skim milk. Adjust
   seasoning with salt and pepper to taste.

Garnish with chopped parsley. For a slightly darker color,
add a few drops of Kitchen Bouquet.

＊SPOTLIGHT (Pages 59, 71)

SPOTLIGHT *shines on homemade soups. What a healthy, satisfying accompaniment for a dinner, for a hearty lunch or Sunday night supper. Soup may easily be made low fat, low cholesterol and salt sparing, so be sensible and soup will bowl you over every time!*

To reduce sodium, use low sodium chicken broth.

YIELD: 12 servings

Nutritive Values (per serving)		calories	187.0 kc
total fat	6.4 g	carbohydrates	16.8 g
monosaturated fat	2.0 g	fiber	0.5 g
polyunsaturated fat	2.7 g	protein	5.2 g
saturated fat	1.1 g	sodium	667.7 mg
cholesterol	2.0 mg	sugar	1.3 g

NAVY BEAN SOUP

2½ cups dried navy beans
1 pound turkey leg, skin removed
3 quarts water
½ teaspoon salt
¼ teaspoon freshly ground pepper
1 bay leaf
⅛ teaspoon ground cloves
1 teaspoon rosemary
1 teaspoon thyme
½ cup parsley, chopped
⅛ teaspoon Tabasco
1 cup coarsely chopped celery and leaves
1½ cups coarsely chopped carrots
1¼ cups coarsely chopped potatoes
1¼ cups coarsely chopped onion

1. Rinse beans. Place in 10 quart soup pot. Cover with water. Soak several hours or overnight. Discard water.

2. Add next 10 ingredients and bring to boil. Reduce heat and simmer covered until beans are tender, 3 to 3½ hours. (Remove turkey leg after 1½ hours. Shred or chop meat.)

3. When beans are tender, return meat to soup along with the remaining vegetables.

4. Simmer 30 minutes more, stirring occasionally. Remove bay leaf.

5. If soup becomes too thick, add small amount of water or chicken broth. Correct seasoning.

VARIATIONS:

Add 3 cups corn kernels.
Use a smoked turkey leg.

YIELD: 18 servings			
Nutritive Values (per serving)		calories	76.3 kc
total fat	1.9 g	carbohydrates	6.3 g
monosaturated fat	0.4 g	fiber	1.2 g
polyunsaturated fat	0.6 g	protein	8.3 g
saturated fat	0.6 g	sodium	91.0 mg
cholesterol	21.4 g	sugar	0.9 g

MARROWFAT BEAN SOUP

Full bodied and thick

1 cup marrowfat beans	¼ teaspoon thyme
8 stalks celery, chopped	¼ teaspoon oregano
5 carrots, chopped	¼ teaspoon basil
1 large or 2 small onions	1 clove garlic, finely chopped
1 tomato	Large ham bone with meat clinging to it or large turkey leg, skin removed
¼-1 teaspoon salt	
Pepper	
A few shakes of paprika, optional	

1. Soak marrowfat beans overnight.

2. Pour off water.

3. Add 2 quarts fresh water. Bring to boil beans, celery, carrots, onions, tomato and seasoning.

4. Add ham bone or turkey leg.

5. Lower heat and simmer 2 hours or until beans are tender (remove turkey when tender). Season to taste.

6. Shred meat and return to soup. Remove fat from surface of soup. For a thicker consistency chop 1 cup of vegetables in food processor with ½ cup of broth. Return to soup and reheat.

Nutritive values calculated using turkey leg.

YIELD: 8 servings

Nutritive Values (per serving)		calories	123.0 kc
total fat	7.8 g	carbohydrates	21.2 g
monosaturated fat	trace	fiber	2.3 g
polyunsaturated fat	0.1 g	protein	8.7 g
saturated fat	trace	sodium	134.0 mg
cholesterol	0.0 mg	sugar	3.8 g

BLACK BEAN SOUP

This is very rich and thick. A little goes a long way.

1 cup black beans	¼ teaspoon ground cloves
8 cups beef stock or water	2 tablespoons sherry
1 carrot, cut in pieces	2 tablespoons lemon juice
1 onion, cut in pieces	Salt and pepper to taste
1 pound turkey leg, skin removed	2 hard cooked egg whites, sliced thin
⅛ teaspoon mace	½ lemon, sliced thin
Dash red pepper	

1. Wash beans, cover with water and soak overnight. In the morning drain water and discard.

2. Chop carrot, onion and 1 cup stock in food processor with several on/off pulses, until coarsely chopped.

3. Pour into large soup pot. Add beans and remaining stock, turkey leg and seasoning. Cover and cook slowly about 3 hours or until beans are very soft. (Remove turkey leg after 2 hours.)

4. Remove meat from bone. Cool soup slightly.

5. Pour soup through a strainer, reserving liquid.

6. Chop meat and vegetables in batches in food processor. Process until smooth.

7. Return puréed mixture and soup to pot. Add sherry and lemon juice; reheat. Correct seasoning.

Place in tureen; top with egg whites and lemon slices.

To reduce sodium, use water rather than beef stock. Correct seasoning at table.

YIELD: 12 servings

Nutritive Values (per serving)		calories	171.0 kc
total fat	3.1 g	carbohydrates	13.8 g
monosaturated fat	0.7 g	fiber	2.5 g
polyunsaturated fat	0.7 g	protein	18.8 g
saturated fat	1.0 g	sodium	565.8 mg
cholesterol	32.8 mg	sugar	1.4 g

CHILI CON CARNE

Ginger snap crumbs for thickening are the secret ingredient. Read the package label for a brand made with healthy oils.

2 pounds ground turkey or chicken	2 teaspoons sugar
¼ cup dehydrated onion or ¾ cup chopped fresh or frozen	2-3 tablespoons chili powder
¼ cup dehydrated green pepper or ¾ cup chopped fresh or frozen	¼ cup chili sauce
1 teaspoon garlic salt or 1 clove chopped garlic	1 28-ounce can tomato sauce

2 pounds ground turkey or chicken
¼ cup dehydrated onion or ¾ cup chopped fresh or frozen
¼ cup dehydrated green pepper or ¾ cup chopped fresh or frozen
1 teaspoon garlic salt or 1 clove chopped garlic

2 teaspoons sugar
2-3 tablespoons chili powder
¼ cup chili sauce
1 28-ounce can tomato sauce
2 28-ounce cans tomato purée
1 28-ounce can kidney beans
½ cup ginger snap crumbs

1. Brown meat; drain off any excess fat. Add next 5 ingredients, stirring to avoid lumps of spices. Add chili sauce, tomato sauce and tomato purée.

2. Simmer 1 hour, stirring occasionally to prevent sticking. Add kidney beans; simmer ½ hour more.

3. Dissolve ginger snap crumbs in ⅓ cup water. Add to chili and simmer 10 minutes. Stir frequently.

Serving suggestions—try our Cincinnati specialties:

CHILI AND SPAGHETTI (use pasta made without egg yolks)

3-WAY: chili, spaghetti, and shredded lite cheddar

4-WAY: chili, spaghetti, shredded lite cheddar and chopped onions

CONEY ISLAND—a chicken or turkey frank in a bun, topped with chili, chopped onions and a sprinkling of lite cheddar

To reduce sodium, use low sodium tomato sauce, tomato purée and kidney beans, and garlic in place of garlic salt.

YIELD: 12 servings

Nutritive Values (per serving)		calories	281.0 kc
total fat	3.0 g	carbohydrates	40.9 g
monosaturated fat	trace	fiber	9.2 g
polyunsaturated fat	0.4 g	protein	26.2 g
saturated fat	0.4 g	sodium	1020.0 mg
cholesterol	43.9 mg	sugar	7.6 g

LENTIL SOUP

Make a double measure and freeze.

1 cup dried lentils
8 cups water
1 onion, chopped
2 cloves garlic, chopped
½ cup diced celery
½ cup sliced carrots
1 teaspoon sugar
½ teaspoon salt
1 teaspoon thyme
¼ teaspoon freshly ground pepper

½ cup chopped fresh parsley (3 tablespoons dried)
2 teaspoons basil
1 teaspoon rosemary
⅛ teaspoon ground cloves
1 bay leaf
2 cups fresh tomatoes, peeled and cubed
4 ounces turkey sausage or turkey franks

1. Soak lentils overnight in water to cover.

2. Drain lentils. Add other ingredients except sausage.

3. Simmer, covered, about 1½ hours or until lentils are tender. Discard bay leaf.

4. Before serving, thin to desired consistency with water. Add sausage, sliced.

To reduce sodium, add salt substitute at table and omit salt.

YIELD: 10 servings

Nutritive Values (per serving)			
total fat	3.0 g	calories	118.0 kc
monosaturated fat	0.0 g	carbohydrates	17.4 g
polyunsaturated fat	0.0 g	fiber	4.2 g
saturated fat	0.0 g	protein	7.3 g
cholesterol	4.7 mg	sodium	241.5 mg
		sugar	3.5 g

MUSHROOM BARLEY SOUP

2½ quarts beef or CHICKEN BROTH (Page 208), fat removed
½ cup chopped onion
1 cup chopped carrot
1 cup chopped celery leaves
⅛ teaspoon pepper
1 16-ounce can tomatoes, chopped
2 stalks celery, cut in pieces
½ cup barley
½ pound chopped mushrooms
Salt or salt substitute to taste

1. Put first 8 ingredients in soup kettle. Bring to boil; cook 2 hours.

2. Add chopped mushrooms during the last half hour.

3. Correct seasoning.

To reduce sodium use low sodium broth and salt substitute. You may also omit celery and celery leaves which are rather high in sodium.

YIELD: 14 servings

Nutritive Values (per serving)		calories	72.0 kc
total fat	1.3 g	carbohydrates	10.4 g
monosaturated fat	0.5 g	fiber	2.2 g
polyunsaturated fat	0.3 g	protein	5.0 g
saturated fat	0.3 g	sodium	705.0 mg
cholesterol	0.7 mg	sugar	2.0 g

CHICKEN MINESTRONE

Keep this soup on hand in your freezer for hurry up meals. With a salad and a loaf of crusty bread, this hearty soup makes a complete meal.

* ¾ cup assorted dried beans
1   small clove garlic
1   bay leaf
10   cups chicken broth, fat removed (CHICKEN BROTH (Page 208))
** 1 3-pound chicken, skin removed
1½ cups canned tomatoes, cut up
2   tablespoons olive oil
½   teaspoon salt
¼   teaspoon freshly ground pepper
¼   cup chopped onion

½   teaspoon dried basil (1½ teaspoons fresh)
1   cup each, sliced carrots, cabbage, and celery with leaves
1   teaspoon dried parsley (1 tablespoon fresh)
1   ounce pasta (without egg yolk)
1   cup raw frozen peas
1   10-ounce package frozen leaf spinach
4   ounces part skim milk mozzarella, shredded

1. Soak beans overnight or 3-4 hours in water to cover; drain and discard water.

2. Tie garlic and bay leaf in a piece of cheesecloth and place in 10 quart soup pot.

3. Add all remaining ingredients except pasta, peas, spinach and mozzarella to beans in pot.

4. Bring to boil, reduce heat and cook slowly, covered, for one hour or until chicken is tender. Remove chicken; take meat from bones; dice and reserve. Continue cooking beans for one hour longer or until tender.

CHICKEN MINESTRONE *(continued)*

5. Remove garlic and bay leaf. Return chicken to soup.

6. Add pasta to boiling soup; cook 5 minutes or until tender.

7. When ready to serve, heat to boiling; add spinach and peas and cook 6 minutes.

Serve with 1 tablespoon mozzarella on top of each bowl of soup.

Refrigerate or freeze until needed. Since the beans may continue to absorb broth, it may be necessary to add additional chicken broth or water for desired consistency.

*This is sometimes marketed as Minestrone Soup Mix. Typically it contains: pinto, black eye, great northern, red, navy, garbanzo, black, lima beans, green split peas, lentils and barley.

**4 cups of leftover chicken or turkey can be used in place of whole chicken. If it is already cooked, add at step 5.

SPOTLIGHT *focuses on legumes, a protein rich, complex carbohydrate. A hill of beans may produce gas. To help alleviate this problem, soak overnight or for several hours. Discard soaking liquid before using beans in recipe. Rinse canned beans to reduce salt. High in fiber, low in fat, sodium and cholesterol, legumes are enjoyable in soups and cold salads.*

To reduce sodium, use low sodium chicken broth.

YIELD: 14 servings			
Nutritive Values (per serving)		calories	244.6 kc
total fat	3.7 g	carbohydrates	14.9 g
monosaturated fat	1.5 g	fiber	1.7 g
polyunsaturated fat	0.6 g	protein	9.9 g
saturated fat	1.1 g	sodium	814.3 mg
cholesterol	61.7 mg	sugar	2.1 g

CHICKEN GUMBO

A low fat, low cholesterol, quick and easy version of a traditional New Orleans gumbo. We have substituted turkey bacon for the real thing. To streamline preparation time, we have used frozen vegetables. (Even the chopped onions can be found in the frozen food department of your supermarket.) In the old days the cook started with a whole, uncooked chicken. Our use of cooked poultry is a tasty way to use leftover chicken or the end of your holiday turkey!

6	strips turkey bacon, chopped		1	clove minced garlic
1½	cups chopped onion		2	tablespoons minced parsley
1	tablespoon vegetable oil		½	cup sliced celery and leaves
*3	tablespoons instant blend flour		3	10-ounce packages frozen succotash (or fordhook lima beans and corn)
10	cups chicken broth, fat removed		4	cups shredded cooked chicken or turkey
3	quarts canned tomatoes		1	tablespoon gumbo filé
3	cups sliced carrots			Salt or salt substitute to taste
2	pounds sliced okra		4	cups cooked brown rice
½	cup chopped green pepper			

1. Fry bacon until crisp. Remove from grease and drain on paper towel. Reserve.

2. In a large soup pot, sauté onion in oil until tender; add flour and continue cooking until lightly browned.

CHICKEN GUMBO *(continued)*

3. Add chicken broth and tomatoes and bring to boil; add next 5 ingredients and cook for 10 minutes. Add celery, succotash and chicken and cook for an additional 10 minutes.

4. When ready to serve, add gumbo filé, stirring to blend. Return to boil. Correct seasoning.

*SPOTLIGHT (Page 94)

Serve over cooked brown rice and top each serving with a few pieces of the fried bacon.

This is a very large recipe. The completed soup and the rice both freeze well.

SPOTLIGHT *on ways to remove fat from homemade soup:*
- *Chill overnight to congeal the fat, then lift it off.*
- *Chill with ice cubes and lift off congealed fat particles that coat the ice.*
- *Remove with a "Magic Mop" gadget.*
- *Soak up fat which has risen to top with paper towels.*
- *The old fashioned way: spoon-off as much of the fat layer as possible. Not as effective as chilling but better than nothing!*

To reduce sodium, omit turkey bacon and use low sodium chicken broth and tomatoes.

YIELD: 12 servings

Nutritive Values (per serving)		calories	304.3 kc
total fat	3.2 g	carbohydrates	56.8 g
monosaturated fat	1.1 g	fiber	5.5 g
polyunsaturated fat	0.8 g	protein	14.1 g
saturated fat	0.5 g	sodium	1086.3 mg
cholesterol	1.7 mg	sugar	13.6 g

MULLIGATAWNY

This recipe, of East Indian origin, was first eaten by British soldiers in India.

⅓ cup finely chopped onion	1 16-ounce can tomatoes, chopped
⅓ cup chopped carrot	1 tablespoon lemon juice
⅓ cup chopped celery	1½ cups shredded, cooked chicken or turkey breast
2 tablespoons chopped green pepper	2 cups tart apple, peeled, cored and chopped
1 tablespoon margarine	1 tablespoon snipped parsley
1 teaspoon sugar	Lime slices for garnish
¼ teaspoon ground cloves	Hot cooked rice (optional)
¾ teaspoon curry powder	
¼ teaspoon salt	
Few grinds pepper	
3 tablespoons flour	
4 cups chicken broth, fat removed	

1. In large saucepan, sauté onion, carrot, celery and green pepper in margarine until wilted.

2. Stir in next 5 ingredients. Continue cooking, stirring occasionally for 5 minutes.

3. Sprinkle flour over vegetable mixture; stir to blend.

4. Add chicken broth, tomatoes and lemon juice; bring to boil, stirring frequently to prevent lumping.

MULLIGATAWNY *(continued)*

5. Add chicken, apple, and parsley. Reduce heat and simmer covered for 15 minutes. Correct seasoning as needed. Garnish with lime slices.

Serve with extra curry powder or one heaping teaspoon MANGO CHUTNEY (Page 237).

For a high fiber nutritious variation, instead of flour, thicken soup with a can of chickpeas or a cup of cooked lentils processed to a smooth paste in food processor.

> **SPOTLIGHT** *on options for soup thickeners (other than flour):*
> - *grind up a portion of the vegetable part of your soup (use your food processor)*
> - *add cooked legumes such as chick peas or navy beans that have been chopped to a pasty consistency (food processor)*
> - *add cooked grains such as rice, barley, quinoa, or couscous, either chopped or unchopped*
> - *add pasta, cooked or uncooked*
> - *add cooked cream of wheat or instant*
> - *add cooked cream of rice or instant*
> - *add dehydrated potatoes*
> - *add cooked puréed white potatoes or sweet potatoes*

For reduced sodium content, substitute low sodium chicken stock and correct seasonings with salt substitute.

YIELD: 10 servings

Nutritive Values (per serving)		calories	123.0 kc
total fat	2.6 g	carbohydrates	10.3 g
monosaturated fat	0.8 g	fiber	1.3 g
polyunsaturated fat	1.0 g	protein	13.4 g
saturated fat	0.5 g	sodium	524.0 mg
cholesterol	29.0 mg	sugar	4.8 g

MUSHROOM TOMATO SOUP WITH SHERRY

1 shallot, chopped	2 11-ounce soup cans water
*½ pound fresh mushrooms, chopped	**1 10¾-ounce can tomato soup
1 teaspoon margarine	2-4 tablespoons sherry (to taste)
2 11-ounce cans beef broth or beef bouillon	

1. Sauté shallots and mushrooms in margarine, using nonstick skillet.

2. Add beef broth, water and tomato soup.

3. Simmer for 10 minutes. Add sherry to taste.

*SPOTLIGHT (Pages 59, 71)

**Do not use a tomato soup that contains cream.

SPOTLIGHT *falls on chicken broth and beef broth. Chill for easy removal of solid fat. Keep a can refrigerated for emergencies. However, be aware that commercial products may be very high in sodium.*

To reduce sodium, use low sodium beef broth and tomato soup, and add seasoned salt substitute.

YIELD: 6 servings

Nutritive Values (per serving)		calories	50.0 kc
total fat	1.5 g	carbohydrates	6.4 g
monosaturated fat	0.4 g	fiber	0.6 g
polyunsaturated fat	0.5 g	protein	2.6 g
saturated fat	0.3 g	sodium	559.0 mg
cholesterol	0.3 mg	sugar	0.8 g

CARROT AND LEEK SOUP

6	large leeks	¼	teaspoon freshly ground pepper
1	pound carrots, peeled and sliced	¼	teaspoon nutmeg
1	tablespoon margarine		Salt or salt substitute to taste
4	cups chicken broth, fat removed		

1. Slice white part of leeks. Discard green leaves. Sauté carrots and leeks in margarine for 5 minutes in large soup pot until vegetables are soft but not brown.

2. Add chicken stock and simmer for about 45 minutes.

3. Purée in food processor and add seasonings.

4. Thin to desired consistency with water or chicken broth.

Make ahead and freeze.

VARIATION: CARROT VICHYSOISSE

Reduce chicken broth to 2 cups. Add 2 cups low fat buttermilk to chilled soup. Enjoy!

SPOTLIGHT *on canned chicken soup: take note that canned chicken soup is extremely high in sodium content.*

To reduce sodium, use salt free chicken broth and salt substitute.

YIELD: 6 servings

Nutritive Values (per serving)		calories	152.0 kc
total fat	3.4 g	carbohydrates	25.9 g
monosaturated fat	1.0 g	fiber	5.0 g
polyunsaturated fat	1.5 g	protein	5.9 g
saturated fat	0.6 g	sodium	683.0 mg
cholesterol	0.7 mg	sugar	9.8 g

QUICK CORN CHOWDER
Comfort food!

⅓	cup grated onion	1	4-ounce can whole corn
2	teaspoons margarine	1	4-ounce can cream style corn
1	14-ounce can chicken broth, undiluted, fat removed	1	cup skim milk Fresh ground pepper

1. Sauté onion in margarine.

2. Add chicken broth. Bring to a boil; simmer 15 minutes. Add corn and milk and heat to boiling point.

Put into hot bowls. Top with ground pepper.

VARIATION:

Add ¾ cup slivered chicken breast or a can of crabmeat, along with the milk.

To reduce sodium, substitute low sodium corn and chicken broth.

YIELD: 3 servings

Nutritive Values (per serving)		calories	123.0 kc
total fat	3.0 g	carbohydrates	16.0 g
monosaturated fat	1.0 g	fiber	1.0 g
polyunsaturated fat	2.0 g	protein	7.0 g
saturated fat	trace	sodium	801.0 mg
cholesterol	2.0 mg	sugar	5.0 g

GREEN PEA SOUP

A delightfully light version of the traditional split pea soup, it is made with frozen peas rather than dried peas. Make in large quantities and freeze for future use.

2	tablespoons chopped onion	½	teaspoon sugar
1	tablespoon margarine	4	tablespoons flour
4	cups frozen peas (20 ounce bag)		Salt and pepper to taste
6	cups chicken broth, fat removed		Few grinds of nutmeg and pinch of thyme (optional)

1. Sauté onion in margarine.

2. Cook peas for 5 minutes in 3 quart pot, with sugar, in 1 cup of chicken broth. Cool a little; purée peas, onions and flour in food processor. Return to cooking pot.

3. Heat remaining chicken broth; gradually stir into pea mixture. Cook over medium heat until thickened, stirring frequently. Correct seasoning.

Serve with pumpernickel rye CROUTONS (Page 252).

SPOTLIGHT on chicken broth: nutrient values of recipes containing chicken broth were computed with commercial chicken broth. If sodium must be limited, make your own (CHICKEN BROTH, Page 208), or use commercially canned low sodium chicken broth.

For reduced sodium content, substitute low sodium chicken broth. Correct seasoning at table.

YIELD: 10 servings

Nutritive Values (per serving)		calories	92.0 kc
total fat	1.3 g	carbohydrates	12.0 g
monosaturated fat	0.3 g	fiber	2.3 g
polyunsaturated fat	0.7 g	protein	6.2 g
saturated fat	0.2 g	sodium	535.0 mg
cholesterol	0.6 mg	sugar	3.6 g

GARDEN SOUP ITALIANO

A light vegetable soup, quick and easy to prepare

1 chopped onion	½ cup sliced celery
1 garlic clove, crushed	¼ teaspoon salt
2 tablespoons margarine	1 teaspoon oregano
3½ cups chicken broth, fat removed	¼ teaspoon basil
	⅛ teaspoon pepper
1 16-ounce can tomatoes, coarsely chopped	2 cups sliced zucchini
	1½ tablespoons Parmesan
½ cup sliced carrots	½ cup CROUTONS (Page 252)

1. Sauté onion and garlic in margarine in soup pot.

2. Add broth, tomatoes, carrots, celery and seasonings. Cover and simmer 15 minutes.

3. Add zucchini. Continue simmering 10 minutes. Garnish with Parmesan and croutons.

To reduce sodium use low sodium chicken soup and correct seasoning at table.

YIELD: 8 servings			
Nutritive Values (per serving)		calories	81.0 kc
total fat	3.5 g	carbohydrates	8.0 g
monosaturated fat	1.0 g	fiber	1.7 g
polyunsaturated fat	1.7 g	protein	4.3 g
saturated fat	0.6 g	sodium	598.0 mg
cholesterol	1.4 mg	sugar	3.0 g

SPEEDY VEGETABLE SOUP

2	tablespoons margarine	½	cup chopped cabbage
4	cups hot water	1	tablespoon chopped parsley (1 teaspoon dried)
½	cup diced carrots		
¼	cup diced onion		
½	cup sliced celery	½	teaspoon salt
1	cup canned tomatoes, chopped	⅛	teaspoon pepper

1. Place all ingredients in pressure cooker.

2. Cook for 3 minutes after control jiggles.

3. Remove from heat and let stand five minutes, then reduce pressure by letting cold water run over pan.

SPOTLIGHT *turns on high for "pressure cookery" which is again in vogue. You not only save time, but retain nutrients as you prepare delicious food. New pressure cookers are improved and the risk of the old pressure blow out has been minimized. The need for added fat is virtually eliminated when you turn up the steam.*

For reduced sodium content use low sodium canned tomatoes.

YIELD: 6 servings

Nutritive Values (per serving)		calories	51.0 kc
total fat	3.9 g	carbohydrates	4.0 g
monosaturated fat	1.4 g	fiber	0.6 g
polyunsaturated fat	1.7 g	protein	0.7 g
saturated fat	0.7 g	sodium	307.0 mg
cholesterol	0.0 mg	sugar	2.1 g

BRUSSELS SPROUT SOUP

2 10-ounce packages frozen Brussels sprouts
1 tablespoon margarine
¼ cup all-purpose flour
¼ teaspoon salt
½ teaspoon pepper

4 cups CHICKEN BROTH (Page 208), fat removed
½ pound fresh mushrooms
2 cups skim milk
2 teaspoons chopped parsley

1. Cook sprouts according to package directions. Drain.

2. Meanwhile, heat margarine in a large saucepan. Blend in the flour, salt, and pepper. Cook until bubbly. Gradually add the broth, stirring to blend. Heat to boiling, stir and boil 1 minute. Remove from heat.

3. Finely chop mushrooms. Mix into hot broth. Cover and simmer 5 minutes.

4. In blender or food processor, purée half of the sprouts with 1 cup of milk. Pour into cooked mushroom mixture. Repeat procedure with remaining sprouts and milk.

5. Heat the soup, stirring occasionally, until serving temperature. Garnish with parsley.

SPOTLIGHT *shines steadily on substitutions. Give consideration to substituting ingredients aimed at lowering fat and cholesterol in all recipes. Look for foods with low calorie content that add fiber and spare the salt. Such vigilence will become routine when it is habitual.*

To reduce sodium use salt free chicken broth. Correct seasoning at table.

YIELD: 8 servings

Nutritive Values (per serving)			
total fat	2.0 g	calories	104.2 kc
monosaturated fat	0.5 g	carbohydrates	12.5 g
polyunsaturated fat	1.0 g	fiber	2.5 g
saturated fat	0.3 g	protein	8.1 g
cholesterol	1.5 mg	sodium	524.0 mg
		sugar	4.5 g

HOT CABBAGE BORSCHT

1 large onion, chopped
1 teaspoon margarine
8 cups CHICKEN
    BROTH (Page 208),
    fat removed, or
    canned broth
1 medium size cabbage
3 tablespoons catsup
⅓ cup sugar
¼ teaspoon pepper

Pinch caraway seeds
1 recipe BASIC
    POULTRY MIX
    (Page 17)
*Instant blend flour
⅓-½ cup lemon juice or
    ½ teaspoon sour
    salt to taste
Salt or salt
    substitute to taste

1. Sauté onion in margarine in nonstick skillet; add to the chicken broth in soup pot.

2. Slice cabbage very thin and add with catsup; bring to a boil.

3. Add next 3 ingredients, simmer, covered for 1 hour.

4. Make small meatballs from the BASIC POULTRY MIX and add to soup. Simmer for ½ hour.

5. If necessary, thicken lightly with instant blend flour.

6. Correct seasoning.

*SPOTLIGHT (Page 94)

To reduce sodium use low sodium chicken broth and catsup.

YIELD: 10 servings

Nutritive Values (per serving)		calories	168.0 kc
total fat	6.0 g	carbohydrates	13.4 g
monosaturated fat	2.0 g	fiber	1.1 g
polyunsaturated fat	2.2 g	protein	13.2 g
saturated fat	1.5 g	sodium	800.0 mg
cholesterol	34.3 mg	sugar	7.7 g

SPINACH SOUP

Delightful Aroma. Enjoy Without Guilt!

6	cups chicken broth, fat removed	½	pound fresh mushrooms, sliced
1	large carrot, thinly sliced	*1	cup tomatoes, peeled, seeded and cubed
1	pound fresh spinach, chopped fine or 1 10-ounce package frozen chopped spinach	2	tablespoons sherry Salt and pepper to taste
		1-2	teaspoons lemon juice
			**Instant blend flour to thicken

1. In medium pan, combine broth and carrot; bring to boil. Simmer 10 minutes.

2. Add mushrooms, spinach and tomatoes. Simmer, covered, 5 minutes more.

3. Add sherry, salt, pepper and lemon juice.

4. Thicken to desired consistency with flour.

Make ahead and freeze.

*SPOTLIGHT (Page 203)

**SPOTLIGHT (Page 94)

VARIATION: SPINACH SOUP ROCKEFELLER

After thickening soup (step 4), add 1 pint oysters and their liquor to boiling soup; return to boil and simmer for 2 minutes. Stir in 2 tablespoons freshly grated Parmesan and 1 or 2 teaspoons anisette (optional).

Nutrient values calculated for SPINACH SOUP. To reduce sodium, use salt free chicken broth and salt substitute.

YIELD: 8 servings

Nutritive Values (per serving)		calories	60.0 kc
total fat	1.3 g	carbohydrates	6.3 g
monosaturated fat	0.5 g	fiber	1.8 g
polyunsaturated fat	0.3 g	protein	5.8 g
saturated fat	0.3 g	sodium	650.0 mg
cholesterol	0.8 mg	sugar	1.8 g

RED SNAPPER CHOWDER

You will be proud to serve this elegant fish chowder to your family and guests. It's a winner!

¼ cup olive oil
¾ cup chopped onion
1 bunch green onions, chopped
1½ cups celery and leaves, sliced
1 green pepper, chopped
⅛ teaspoon each:
   soy sauce,
   garlic powder,
   cayenne pepper
1 tablespoon curry powder
1 tablespoon Hungarian paprika

*2 cups fresh tomatoes, peeled and chopped or canned Italian plum tomatoes, chopped
1 46-ounce can tomato juice
1 cup dry white wine
2½ pounds red snapper (or orange roughy) cut into 1 inch cubes
1 cup skim milk
½ cup chopped parsley
1-2 tablespoons flour
¼ cup dry sherry

1. Heat olive oil in large soup pot; add onion, green onions, celery and green pepper. Sauté until transparent.

2. Add spices, tomatoes, tomato juice and wine; bring to boil; reduce heat and simmer 25 minutes. Add fish and continue cooking for 20 minutes. Flake fish and return to pot.

3. Add skim milk and parsley. Dissolve flour in sherry. Add to soup, stirring carefully to prevent lumps forming. Boil for 2 minutes to thicken.

*SPOTLIGHT (Page 203)

To reduce sodium content substitute low sodium soy sauce, canned tomatoes, and tomato juice.

YIELD: 10 servings

Nutritive Values (per serving)		calories	245.7 kc
total fat	7.4 g	carbohydrates	13.8 g
monosaturated fat	4.3 g	fiber	3.1 g
polyunsaturated fat	1.2 g	protein	26.3 g
saturated fat	1.2 g	sodium	720.0 mg
cholesterol	41.8 mg	sugar	7.5 g

FISH SOUP WITH CHUNKY VEGETABLES

Remember, fish is not only brain food, it's heart food!

2½ quarts water
4 carrots, cut in ½ inch slices
2 cups celery and leaves, sliced
2 medium onions, chopped
2 cups potatoes, peeled and cut in chunks
1 15-ounce can stewed tomatoes, cut in chunks

2 tablespoons olive oil
¾ teaspoon freshly ground pepper
1 tablespoon fresh basil (1 teaspoon dried)
2½ pounds cod or haddock
*Instant blend flour to thicken (optional)
Salt and pepper to taste

1. Place first 9 ingredients in soup pot. Bring to boil and simmer for 25 minutes.

2. Add fish and simmer 15 minutes more.

3. If desired, thicken lightly. Add salt and pepper to taste.

Fill your soup mugs and enjoy! Serve with CRACKERS (Page 138) or PITA TRIANGLES (Page 255) or TORTILLA CRAX (Page 255).

*SPOTLIGHT (Page 94)

YIELD: 12 servings			
Nutritive Values (per serving)		calories	170.5 kc
total fat	3.7 g	carbohydrates	13.0 g
monosaturated fat	1.9 g	fiber	1.9 g
polyunsaturated fat	0.7 g	protein	20.8 g
saturated fat	0.6 g	sodium	145.8 mg
cholesterol	34.5 mg	sugar	3.5 g

FISH SOUP MELANGE

A great formula for transforming leftovers into gourmet fare.
Accumulate your leftovers in plastic containers in freezer.

USE:

Broth drained from:

MUSSELS POACHED IN GARLIC WINE SAUCE
(Page 89)

SALMON POACHED IN COOKING BAG (Page 102)

Broth drained from canned salmon

Additional stock or bouillon (allow ¾ cup liquid per serving)

Leftover:

Cooked vegetables

Rice or wild rice

Pieces of any leftover cooked fish

Shrimp, scallops, clams or oysters

1. Bring liquid ingredients to boil and simmer for 5 minutes.

2. Add solid ingredients and additional stock to reach
   desired consistency. Return to boil and simmer
   2 minutes.

3. Correct seasoning.

Serve with a loaf of hot herb bread.

Nutritive values will vary with selection of ingredients.

♥ ZUPPA di POMODORI

A hearty soup, thickened with Italian bread cubes and sparked by the flavors of fresh basil and ripe plum tomatoes. A drizzle of olive oil on the surface of each bowl gives the suggestion of richness to a dish that is surprisingly low in fat.

1   clove garlic
2   cups canned plum tomatoes in tomato purée, chopped
½   cup dry white wine
1-2 teaspoons sugar to taste
⅛   teaspoon freshly ground pepper
*2   cups (1¼ pounds) fresh ripe plum tomatoes, peeled, seeded and coarsely chopped.

1   tablespoon chopped cilantro or parsley
2   teaspoons chopped basil (½ teaspoon dried)
**1½ cups (3 ounces) French or Italian bread, crusts removed and cut into ⅜ inch cubes
2   tablespoons Parmesan, divided
Olive oil for garnish
10 whole fresh basil leaves

1. Peel garlic; pierce in several places and spear with a toothpick.

2. Simmer first 4 ingredients for 10 minutes.

3. Add fresh tomatoes, cilantro and chopped basil; bring back to boil, reduce heat and simmer for 5 minutes.

4. Add bread cubes and 1 tablespoon Parmesan. Continue cooking for 5 minutes more. Remove garlic clove.

ZUPPA di POMODORI *(continued)*

5. Pour piping hot into bowls. Garnish each bowl with ½ teaspoon Parmesan, 2 small basil leaves and a few drops of olive oil.

**This is a good use for the insides of a loaf of bread prepared for PIZZA LOAF (Page 230). For a substantial fish soup, add clams, mussels and shrimp to boiling soup, return to boil and simmer 2 minutes (or until clam and mussel shells open).

VARIATION: for a more substantial soup, add clams, mussels, oysters or shrimp (or combination of all) to boiling soup, return to boil and simmer 2 minutes (or until clam and mussel shells open). See SPOTLIGHT on cleaning mussels (Page 89).

__SPOTLIGHT__ on tomatoes: store at room temperature to preserve flavor. To peel and prepare tomatoes: place in pot of boiling water for 10 seconds. (Plum tomatoes may require up to 30 seconds.) Remove from water; slip skin off. To extract juice and seeds, cut in half, crosswise and squeeze.

YIELD: 6 servings

Nutritive Values (per serving)		calories	109.0 kc
total fat	2.3 g	carbohydrates	16.4 g
monosaturated fat	0.8 g	fiber	2.2 g
polyunsaturated fat	0.2 g	protein	3.9 g
saturated fat	0.6 g	sodium	267.2 mg
cholesterol	1.6 mg	sugar	6.0 g

HOT AND SOUR SOUP

8 cups CHICKEN BROTH (Page 208), or commercial chicken broth, fat removed

2 tablespoons vinegar

2 teaspoons soy sauce
Few grinds pepper

1-2 teaspoons Tabasco

1 teaspoon sesame oil

2 tablespoons cornstarch, dissolved in ¼ cup water

*1 pound thinly sliced mushrooms

½ cup sliced bamboo shoots

½ cup slivered water chestnuts

1 cup POACHED CHICKEN BREAST (Page 29), cut in very thin strips (¾ pound chicken breast)

**8 ounces extra firm tofu, cut in small cubes or slices

2 egg whites, beaten with one tablespoon of water

½ cup scallions, thinly sliced (use white and green)

1. Bring chicken broth to a boil.

2. Add next 5 ingredients and simmer 2 minutes.

3. Add dissolved cornstarch; simmer for 2 minutes, stirring constantly.

4. Add vegetables, chicken and tofu. Simmer 2 minutes.

5. Bring soup to rapid boil. Stir raw egg white mixture into boiling broth with fork. Boil no longer than 1 minute more.

HOT AND SOUR SOUP *(continued)*

6. Pour into serving bowls. Garnish with sliced scallions.

Prepare soup in advance through step 4. Proceed with recipe at serving time.

＊SPOTLIGHT (Pages 59, 71)

＊＊SPOTLIGHT (Page 69)

SPOTLIGHT *focuses on lite soy sauce: there is less sodium than in the regular product with very little loss in flavor. Fine china for a grain of salt!*

To reduce sodium substitute low sodium chicken broth and soy sauce. Additionally, rinse bamboo shoots and water chestnuts.

YIELD: 10 servings			
Nutritive Values (per serving)		calories	170.0 kc
total fat	4.3 g	carbohydrates	6.8 g
monosaturated fat	1.3 g	fiber	1.1 g
polyunsaturated fat	1.8 g	protein	15.7 g
saturated fat	0.8 g	sodium	721.1 mg
cholesterol	17.9 mg	sugar	0.7 g

 STEW SOUP

We hate to throw them out, so they seem to accumulate in our refrigerators and freezers. Remember, that with a few creative additions, leftovers make great soups.

SUGGESTED INGREDIENTS

**Leftover stew meat and vegetables
Leftover noodles, rice, barley or other grain
Broth, stock, or reconstituted bouillon cubes and water
to accommodate your leftover meat and vegetables.**

1. Chop stew coarsely in food processor using steel blade, with rapid on/off motions.

2. Place in pot with enough broth to thin to desired consistency. Add any other ingredients you have on hand.

3. Bring to boil and simmer for 10 minutes.

4. Correct seasoning.

Serve with CORNY CORN MUFFINS (Page 257)

MOCK TURTLE SOUP

2	pounds lean ground turkey	5	cups water, divided
¾	cup chopped onion	*1	cup ginger snap crumbs (about 20 ginger snaps)
1	clove garlic, chopped		Salt or salt substitute to taste
1	14-ounce bottle catsup		Dash pepper
½	cup Worcestershire sauce		Whites of 3 hard boiled eggs
1	lemon, seeded and sliced paper-thin		Sherry
2	tablespoons cider vinegar		

1. Brown ground turkey in large soup pot, lightly greased. Use a potato masher to separate pieces of meat. Add onion and garlic and cook for 5 minutes, stirring frequently.

2. Add next 5 ingredients, reserving 1 cup water. Simmer soup for 1 hour.

3. Stir in ginger-snap crumbs that have been mixed with remaining cup of water. Cook, stirring constantly for 5-10 minutes. Correct seasoning with salt and pepper to taste.

4. Add chopped egg whites and a dash of sherry to each dish.

*Read ginger snap label carefully to avoid cookies that contain animal fat.

YIELD: 14 servings

Nutritive Values (per serving)		calories	191.0 kc
total fat	8.1 g	carbohydrates	17.7 g
monosaturated fat	2.3 g	fiber	0.2 g
polyunsaturated fat	1.6 g	protein	12.8 g
saturated fat	2.1 g	sodium	491.0 mg
cholesterol	47.9 mg	sugar	6.9 g

CHICKEN BROTH

TRADITIONAL METHOD

5	pounds chicken backs, necks, wings, bones	¼-½	chopped onion (1 tablespoon dehydrated onion flakes)
	Water to cover		
8	peppercorns		
8	whole cloves	½	cup celery leaves

1. Place all of the above in 8 quart soup pot. Simmer 2-3 hours.

2. Strain broth.

3. Chill; remove and discard hardened fat. Freeze in pint containers for use in recipes requiring chicken broth or as a base for soups. Correct seasonings as needed for specific usage.

BROTH IN BAG

Place all the above ingredients in a Reynolds™ Oven Cooking Bag. Reduce water to 4 cups. Close bag according to manufacturer's instructions. Place bag in 2 inch deep baking pan in 350° oven for 1¼ hours. This method produces a concentrated stock, saves time and potwashing. SPOTLIGHT (Page 103)

FEATHERED CHICKEN BROTH

Chinese restaurants often feature FEATHERED CHICKEN BROTH. How easy it is to prepare! Bring completed CHICKEN BROTH (above) to a boil. For each 4 cups of broth, whisk in 1 egg white beaten with ½ teaspoon water. Boil no longer than 1 minute more. See HOT AND SOUR SOUP (Page 204) for a delicious variation.

Nutritive values of above soups will vary with concentration of broth and amount of salt added.

QUICK AND EASY GAZPACHO

1   46-ounce can seasoned tomato juice
1   medium cucumber, peeled, seeded and cut into chunks
1   small green pepper, seeded and quartered
2   stalks celery and leaves
1/2   medium onion, cut in half

1   clove garlic
2   tablespoons olive oil
2   tablespoons red wine vinegar or part herb vinegar
2   teaspoons Worcestershire sauce
     Freshly ground pepper (optional)
     Snipped fresh chives

1. Process 2 cups of the tomato juice with all remaining ingredients except pepper in food processor, using steel knife to make coarse consistency. Add remaining tomato juice.

2. Add freshly ground pepper to taste. Chill.

Serve with snipped chives and plain or garlic CROUTONS (Page 252).

For extra crunch, add a generous spoonful of your own freshly made PLUM TOMATO SALSA (Page 240) to each serving.

YIELD: 8 servings

Nutritive Values (per serving)			
total fat	3.5 g	calories	74.9 kc
monosaturated fat	2.5 g	carbohydrates	9.4 g
polyunsaturated fat	0.3 g	fiber	0.8 g
saturated fat	0.5 g	protein	2.2 g
cholesterol	0.0 mg	sodium	955.0 mg
		sugar	6.7 g

TOMATO REFRESHER

3	cups seasoned tomato juice	1/4	cup celery, coarsely chopped
3/4	cup low fat yogurt		Green onion to garnish
1/2	cucumber, coarsely chopped (remove skin if it appears waxed)		Freshly ground pepper

1. Blend tomato juice and yogurt.

2. Add cucumber and celery to tomato juice.

3. Chill soup.

4. Garnish with thinly sliced onion and pepper when serving.

Serve in chilled mugs.

For reduced sodium content, substitute low sodium tomato juice and a low sodium herb salt to taste.

YIELD: 6 servings			
Nutritive Values (per serving)		calories	48.0 kc
total fat	0.5 g	carbohydrates	9.0 g
monosaturated fat	0.1 g	fiber	0.4 g
polyunsaturated fat	trace	protein	2.9 g
saturated fat	0.3 g	sodium	674.0 mg
cholesterol	1.7 mg	sugar	6.0 g

TOMATO SOUP AL FRESCO

This delightful summer soup is similar to gazpacho yet more delicate and unusual. Make in season with vine ripened tomatoes fresh from the garden. The seasoning of the soup may vary depending on the taste of the chef.

*6   medium sized tomatoes (approximately 4 cups), peeled
2   medium sized shallots, quartered
¼   cup fresh lemon juice
1   tablespoon olive oil
3   drops Tabasco
¼   teaspoon salt

     Ground black pepper
½-1   teaspoon sugar or sugar substitute to taste
**6   tablespoons low fat yogurt drained 20 minutes
½   teaspoon curry powder

1. Cut up tomatoes and process in food processor with shallots for a few seconds, until you have a coarse purée and the seeds are ground up.

2. Add the lemon juice, oil, Tabasco, salt, pepper and sugar to taste.

3. Chill for at least eight hours.

4. When ready to serve, mix yogurt with curry powder and salt and pepper to taste. Place the soup in bowls and garnish by floating a tablespoon of the seasoned yogurt in each bowl.

*SPOTLIGHT (Page 203)

**ALL ABOUT YOGURT (Page 154)

YIELD: 4 servings

Nutritive Values (per serving)		calories	98.6 kc
total fat	4.2 g	carbohydrates	14.3 g
monosaturated fat	2.6 g	fiber	1.2 g
polyunsaturated fat	0.5 g	protein	3.4 g
saturated fat	0.8 g	sodium	167.5 mg
cholesterol	1.3 mg	sugar	7.8 g

CRÊME de CRAB

A refreshing cold buttermilk based seafood soup

½ bunch green onions (5 medium)
½ green pepper
1 cucumber, peeled and seeded
1 zucchini
¼ cup celery, chopped
¼ cup parsley, chopped
¼ cup watercress, chopped
*½ cup dill pickle, chopped

½ cup low fat yogurt
1 quart low fat buttermilk
½ teaspoon salt
1 teaspoon dill weed
Dash of garlic powder and black pepper
**2 cups mock crab (bite size pieces) or lump crabmeat

1. Mix all ingredients except seafood.

2. Process in batches in blender or food processor until smooth.

3. Chill thoroughly.

4. Just before serving, add crabmeat.

Make a day ahead. Serve from tureen in chilled mugs.

*DILL PICKLE NUTRITIVE CHART (Page 141)

**SPOTLIGHT (Pages 95, 105)

The dill pickle contributes most of the sodium.

YIELD: 8 servings

Nutritive Values (per serving)			
total fat	1.0 g	calories	70.0 kc
monosaturated fat	1.1 g	carbohydrates	10.0 g
polyunsaturated fat	trace	fiber	1.3 g
saturated fat	0.6 g	protein	5.7 g
cholesterol	9.2 mg	sodium	418.5 mg
		sugar	1.9 g

JELLIED MADRILÈNE

2 cans madrilène	¼ cup low fat yogurt, drained for 5 minutes on paper towels
¼ cup chopped green olives	Capers
1 cup diced tomatoes, well drained	

1. Chill madrilène until practically jelled.

2. Fold in well drained tomatoes and olives.

3. Pour into soup cups.

4. Top each cup with 1 tablespoon yogurt and sprinkle with capers.

This is a mild, delicately flavored soup. For a more highly seasoned soup you may also add:

½ cup finely chopped green pepper

2 tablespoons finely chopped shallot

Tabasco to taste

*ALL ABOUT YOGURT (Page 154)

YIELD: 4 servings

Nutritive Values (per serving)		calories	81.0 kc
total fat	4.5 g	carbohydrates	6.7 g
monosaturated fat	1.3 g	fiber	1.7 g
polyunsaturated fat	0.2 g	protein	5.7 g
saturated fat	2.2 g	sodium	785.0 mg
cholesterol	0.0 g	sugar	2.3 g

JELLIED CLAMATO SOUP

2   cans madrilène
1   10-ounce can minced clams, well-drained
¼   cup low fat yogurt, drained 5 minutes on paper
      towels
    Capers (optional)

1. Chill madrilène until practically jelled.

2. Fold in well-drained clams. Pour into mugs.

3. Top with 1 tablespoon yogurt and sprinkle with capers.

*ALL ABOUT YOGURT (Page 154)

YIELD: 4 servings

Nutritive Values (per serving)		calories	62.5 kc
total fat	0.9 g	carbohydrates	3.6 g
monosaturated fat	trace	fiber	0.3 g
polyunsaturated fat	trace	protein	9.2 g
saturated fat	trace	sodium	612.0 mg
cholesterol	44.8 mg	sugar	0.1 g

9

PIZZA AND PASTA POSITIVELY

PASTA POINTERS

SPOTLIGHT *nixes the "villain" idea about pasta and changes it into a dietary friend. Excessive calories and fat come from the sauce ingredients, not the pasta. High in complex carbohydrates, fiber rich whole wheat pasta is the healthiest. (It doesn't taste so great, though!) And read the labels: buy eggless.*

SPOTLIGHT *on cooking pasta: use at least one quart of boiling water for every 4 ounces of dry pasta. Stir frequently to prevent sticking. Cooking time varies for each type of pasta. Very thin angel hair pasta can cook in 1 to 2 minutes, while thicker pasta may require up to 20 minutes. Remember the Italian description, al dente (to the tooth) and do not overcook. Handle each type of pasta as directed by manufacturer for best results. Pasta lovers, enjoy!*

SPOTLIGHT *advises you to stop the cooking process by adding 2 cups of cold water to pot of cooked pasta before draining. Drain pasta into a colander or strainer without rinsing. A small amount of sauce mixed into the freshly drained pasta prevents sticking.*

SPOTLIGHT *on leftover pasta: toss with a small amount of oil to coat; cover and refrigerate up to 3 days. To reheat, place in boiling water; stir to separate; return to boil and cook for 1 minute. You may also freeze leftover pasta. To reheat, add to boiling water; stir to separate; return to boil and cook for 2 minutes. Pasta may alternately be reheated briefly in a microwave oven. Follow your microwave instructions to avoid overcooking.*

BAKING HEALTHY PIZZAS

Pizza is heart food! The crust, vegetables, olive oil and part skim milk cheese are a healthy source of protein, calcium, monounsaturated fats, and complex carbohydrates.

The goal of **BEGINNING LIGHT**'s pizza chapter is to help you produce, with ease, *a healthy hors d'oeuvre*, one with a *crisp crust underneath* and a *layer of creamy cheese on top.*

It is interesting to note that a thick crust produces a healthier, lower fat product than the thin type. There is a larger percentage of complex carbohydrate in relation to the fat and cholesterol in the thicker crust pizza. So don't spare the crust!

Consider the following suggestions of pizza making options. They make 12-13 inch deep-dish or flat pizzas (12 slices). You might also try your pizza in a rectangular jelly roll pan (10½ × 15½) and cut your pie in squares.

YOUR CHOICE OF CRUSTS

TRADITIONAL PIZZA DOUGH (Page 218)

FOOD PROCESSOR PIZZA DOUGH (Page 218)

Frozen commercial white or whole wheat bread dough— Rhodes™ or Rich's™ are suggested brands. Read labels carefully to avoid harmful fats and egg yolks.

Bakery French or Italian bread dough, unbaked

Commercially baked French or Italian bread loaves (scoop 'em out!) (PIZZA LOAF, Page 230)

Tortillas

English muffins, sliced horizontally into thirds

Pita breads, halved (try healthy whole wheat pita)

Bagel halves

Boboli, a pre-baked, chewy flatbread

FOOD PROCESSOR PIZZA DOUGH

You can't miss with this method!

1 package dry yeast	*2½ cups bread flour or
¼ cup warm water (110°)	1¼ cups bread
1 teaspoon sugar	flour and 1¼ cups
⅛ teaspoon ginger	whole wheat flour
½ teaspoon salt	½-¾ cup cold water
2 tablespoons olive oil	Olive oil spray

1. To proof yeast: place yeast, warm water, ginger and sugar in an 8-ounce glass or 1 cup measure; stir to blend. Set in warm place until it bubbles, about 5 minutes.

2. Place flour and salt in food processor bowl with steel blade or yeast blade. Turn on and immediately off to blend.

3. Add olive oil and yeast mixture; turn on/off twice.

4. With machine running, add cold water until a ball forms. Process one minute. If ball feels too sticky to handle, add flour, 1 tablespoon at a time, running machine just long enough to incorporate flour. Let dough rest 5 minutes.

5. Place ball of dough in an ungreased 2 quart bowl; spray top of dough with olive oil spray. Cover with damp cloth. Let rise in warm spot until double in bulk. Knead for 5 minutes. Cover dough and allow to rest for 10 minutes while you prepare pan (Page 219).

TRADITIONAL METHOD PIZZA DOUGH

1. Follow step 1 as above.

2. Place yeast mixture, 1 cup water, oil and salt in mixing bowl. Stir to blend. Beat mixture, at same time adding flour, ½ cup at a time, until dough begins to leave sides of bowl.

3. Spread ¾ cup flour on counter top or any flat surface. Pour dough onto flour. Let dough rest 10 minutes.

4. Knead dough until smooth and satiny, incorporating only enough additional flour to prevent sticking to work surface.

Continue as in step 5 above.

PREPARING THE PAN:

Spray a 12- or 13-inch pan with olive oil; sprinkle with 2 teaspoons cornmeal.

ROLLING THE DOUGH:

1. Place dough on lightly floured surface. Roll into circle. Lift, turn over and roll again. Allow to rest 5 minutes. Repeat until dough stretches into a circle large enough to overhang pan ¾ inch all the way around.

2. Ease circle of dough into pan. **For deep dish pizza,** press dough to pan contours, allowing ¾ inch to 1 inch up the sides. **For flat pan pizza,** turn dough edge over to form lip. (Use a 9x13-inch rectangular pan if you plan to cut pizza into squares.)

3. Prick surface lightly with fork, not all the way to bottom.

4. Spray with olive oil spray.

 ## PREBAKING THE CRUST:

*To guarantee a crisp crust, **prebake crust as follows,** then fill baked crust with sauce and toppings.*

1. Place crust on bottom shelf of preheated 400° oven; Bake for 12-14 minutes. Top of crust will be lightly browned, bottom slightly darker.

2. Cool on wire rack. The crust is now ready to fill or freeze. Remember to thaw pre-baked pizza crust before filling. Cover surface with a sheet of waxed paper or a towel to prevent condensation of moisture on surface of dough.

YOUR CHOICE OF SAUCES:

FRESH TOMATO PIZZA SAUCE (Page 239)

Commercial pizza sauce. Read labels carefully to avoid excessive salt, sugar and harmful oils.

Combination: half pizza sauce and half tomato sauce

PESTO SUPREME (Page 241)

RATATOUILLE SALAD (Page 54)

YOUR CHOICE OF TOPPINGS:

It's the harmful, fat-laden toppings, not the pizza crust which give pizza a high calorie, high cholesterol reputation. Here are some HEARTSMART topping options:

CHEESES:

BEGINNING LIGHT recommends that your pizza's final layer of cheese is heated only the briefest amount of time, just enough to melt, so that it remains creamy and smooth. Otherwise it becomes "rubbery."

Recommended: (cheeses containing less than 6 grams of fat per ounce)
    Part skim milk mozzarella
    Parmesan, used in small quantities
    Tofu mozzarella

VEGETABLES:

Broccoli, chopped or small flowerets
Cauliflower flowerets
Green, red or yellow pepper rings
Jalapeño peppers, thinly sliced
Mushrooms, freshly sliced
Onion, chopped or rings
RATATOUILLE SALAD (Page 54)
Shredded carrots
Spinach
Tomatoes, fresh
Tomatoes, sun dried (Page 157)

MEATS:

The healthiest pizza is meatless, but sometimes we cater to our less healthy selves!

Beef, lean ground
Pork, lean ground
Poultry, lean ground
Tiny meatballs (BASIC GROUND POULTRY MIX, Page 17)
Canadian bacon or lean ham, cubed

HERBS AND SPICES:

Fresh herbs provide the best flavor, but dried herbs can be substituted. A rule of thumb is to use 3 times as much fresh as dried.

Basil
Cumin
Garlic
Hot red pepper flakes (sprinkle over baked pizza)
Oregano
Sesame, poppy or caraway seeds

 ## BAKING THE PIZZA:

Remember, our aim is to insure a crisp crust underneath, then a layer of "creamy" cheese on top.

1. Preheat oven to 450°.

2. Place a large pan on top shelf of oven to diffuse heat.

3. Place pizza on bottom shelf of oven.

4. *To prevent toughening of part skim milk mozzarella, sprinkle top layer of mozzarella over pizza during the final 2-3 minutes of baking time, just until cheese melts.*

5. When baking is completed, remove pizza from pan; cool on wire rack for 5 minutes. Place on platter to cut and serve.

CUTTING THE PIZZA:

Use a kitchen scissors or a pizza cutting wheel for neat slices.

YOUR CHOICE OF BAKING EQUIPMENT:

Follow manufacturer's instructions for precise baking time and temperature.

Shallow or deep dish nonstick 12-13 inch round pizza baking pan

Rectangular baking pan ($10\frac{1}{2} \times 15\frac{1}{2}$ inches) with sides

A perforated pizza pan is another good choice. The perforations allow hot air to reach the exposed part of the crust.

Aluminum mesh pizza screen

A pizza stone, which works like a brick oven; you may purchase one in most cookware stores. The stone is preheated in the oven. Then the assembled pizza is slid from a flat cookie sheet onto it. (Be sure that you have sprinkled the cookie sheet with corn meal for easy sliding.)

PIZZA

Makes 12 slices

1	12- or 13-inch deep dish or flat prebaked pizza crust (BAKING HEALTHY PIZZAS, Pages 217-219)
	Olive oil spray
2	teaspoons corn meal
	Toppings of your choice (TOPPINGS, Page 220)
¾-1	cup FRESH TOMATO PIZZA SAUCE (Page 239) or canned pizza sauce
10	ounces part skim milk mozzarella, shredded
2	tablespoons Parmesan

1. Prepare pan, roll dough and prebake according to GENERAL INSTRUCTIONS (Page 219).

2. Spread half of mozzarella over dough, leaving a ½ inch border. Spread pizza sauce evenly over cheese. Arrange assortment of toppings on sauce. Sprinkle with Parmesan and spray lightly with olive oil.

3. Place a large flat pan on top shelf of preheated 400° oven to diffuse heat. Place pizza on lowest shelf of preheated 400° oven. Bake for 15-18 minutes or until crust is nicely browned on bottom.

4. Sprinkle remaining mozzarella over pizza and return to oven long enough to melt cheese, approximately 2-3 minutes.

5. Remove cooled pizza from pan; cool on wire rack for 5 minutes. Place on platter to cut and serve.

VARIATION: RATATOUILLE PIZZA

Substitute 1 cup RATATOUILLE SALAD (Page 54) for pizza sauce or FRESH TOMATO PIZZA SAUCE (Page 239).

The nutritive analysis is for PIZZA, based on 1 recipe FOOD PROCESSOR PIZZA DOUGH (Page 218).

YIELD: 12 slices			
Nutritive Values (per slice)		calories	180.3 kc
total fat	5.8 g	carbohydrates	22.8 g
monosaturated fat	2.6 g	fiber	1.2 g
polyunsaturated fat	0.3 g	protein	8.4 g
saturated fat	2.5 g	sodium	203.3 mg
cholesterol	11.6 mg	sugar	0.8 g

♥SPINOCCOLI PIZZA

A vegetable delight—so delicious and simple to create!

1   prebaked 12-13-inch pizza crust (BAKING
      HEALTHY PIZZAS, Pages 217-219)

2   teaspoons olive oil

1   large clove garlic, finely chopped

1   10-ounce package frozen broccoli flowerets, thawed
      and drained on a paper towel

1   10-ounce package frozen chopped spinach, thawed
      and wrung dry

1   dozen basil leaves, chopped ($\frac{1}{2}$ teaspoon dried)
      Olive oil spray

10 ounces part skim milk mozzarella, shredded

1   cup FRESH TOMATO PIZZA SAUCE (Page 239), or
      commercial pizza sauce

1   tablespoon Parmesan

$\frac{1}{2}$ red pepper in $\frac{1}{4}$-inch strips (optional garnish)

$\frac{1}{2}$ yellow pepper in $\frac{1}{4}$-inch strips (optional garnish)

1. Sauté chopped garlic in 1 teaspoon olive oil for $\frac{1}{2}$
minute. *Do not* let it brown.

2. Combine sautéed garlic, broccoli, spinach, basil and
remaining olive oil.

3. Spray top side of pizza crust with olive oil spray.

4. Spread $\frac{3}{4}$ cup mozzarella over crust.

5. Spread pizza sauce over cheese.

6. Spread vegetable mixture over all.

7. Sprinkle with Parmesan.

SPINOCCOLI PIZZA *(continued)*

8. Arrange strips of red pepper or yellow pepper on surface of pizza. (This is optional but adds to an attractive presentation.)

9. Spray with olive oil.

10. Cut out circle of foil and loosely cover vegetables, not crust.

11. Preheat oven to 450°. Place a large pan on top shelf of oven to diffuse heat. Place pizza on bottom shelf of oven and bake for 20 minutes.

12. Remove foil. Sprinkle remaining mozzarella over pizza. Return to oven for 2 or 3 minutes or until cheese melts. Cool on wire rack for 5 minutes before serving. Slice to serve.

SPOTLIGHT *doesn't fade away when it sees pizza on the menu. New techniques make a former diet "no-no" into a low fat "yes." Pizza is okay. Don't pan it.*

The nutritive analysis is based on 1 recipe FOOD PROCESSOR PIZZA DOUGH (Page 218).

YIELD: 12 slices

Nutritive Values (per slice)		calories	222.4 kc
total fat	8.3 g	carbohydrates	26.6 g
monosaturated fat	3.8 g	fiber	2.3 g
polyunsaturated fat	0.7 g	protein	10.8 g
saturated fat	3.2 g	sodium	335.7 mg
cholesterol	13.9 mg	sugar	1.2 g

ONION PIZZA

1   12- or 13-inch prebaked pizza crust, read BAKING
    HEALTHY PIZZAS (Pages 217-219)
    Olive oil spray
1   pound sweet onions,
    sliced very thin
1   tablespoon olive oil
⅛   teaspoon freshly
    ground pepper
1 egg white

2   tablespoons
    Parmesan, divided
⅛   teaspoon coarse salt
    Poppy seeds
    Caraway seeds
    Sesame seeds

1. Spread onions in oil-sprayed baking dish; sprinkle with
   1 tablespoon olive oil; cover loosely with a sheet of
   waxed paper and microwave for 6-8 minutes, or until
   tender. Rotate dish and stir onions after 4 minutes. (The
   onions may also be sautéed in a nonstick skillet.)

2. Beat egg white lightly with pepper; mix with onions and
   add 1 tablespoon Parmesan.

3. Spray cooled crust lightly with olive oil. Spread onions
   evenly over crust. Sprinkle with remaining Parmesan and
   salt. Decorate by sprinkling alternating rows of the seeds
   over onions. Spray lightly with olive oil spray.

4. Place a large pan on top shelf of preheated 400° oven to
   diffuse heat. Place pizza on bottom shelf of oven and
   bake for 15 minutes.

5. Cool on large wire rack for 5 minutes before slicing to
   serve.

Prepare in advance, cool, wrap and refrigerate or freeze.
Reheat when ready to serve.

Nutritive analysis calculated with FOOD PROCESSOR PIZZA
DOUGH.

YIELD: 12 slices

Nutritive Values (per slice)		calories	147.5 kc
total fat	4.1 g	carbohydrates	23.3 g
monosaturated fat	2.6 g	fiber	1.5 g
polyunsaturated fat	0.4 g	protein	4.2 g
saturated fat	0.7 g	sodium	135.7 mg
cholesterol	0.8 mg	sugar	1.8 g

PITA PIZZAS

1   pita bread
    Olive oil spray
½   cup (2 ounces) shredded part skim milk mozzarella
2-3 tablespoons FRESH TOMATO PIZZA SAUCE
        (Page 239) or commercial pizza sauce
½   teaspoon Parmesan

1. Separate pita into two thin discs by cutting around edge
   with scissors or sharp knife. Place on cookie sheet,
   inside surface up. Spray with olive oil spray. Bake in
   preheated 375° oven for 7-8 minutes to brown.

2. Cover with 2 tablespoons mozzarella (1 tablespoon each
   disc). Spread with pizza sauce, then sprinkle with
   Parmesan; spray lightly with olive oil.

3. Bake in preheated 375° oven for 6 minutes. Remove
   from oven and sprinkle with remaining mozzarella.
   Return to oven for 1-2 minutes until cheese melts.

4. Remove from oven. Cut each disc into quarters.

VARIATION: PESTO PITA PIZZA

¼   cup PESTO SUPREME (Page 241)
6   sun dried tomatoes, reconstituted in water and
        slivered, or ½ cup plum tomatoes, peeled,
        drained and cubed
½   teaspoon Parmesan
    Olive oil spray
½   cup shredded part skim milk mozzarella cheese
    Olives, green pepper, onion, capers, mushrooms

Spread 2 tablespoons PESTO on each disk; sprinkle with
tomato pieces and ¼ teaspoon Parmesan. Spray lightly
with olive oil. Continue as in steps 4 and 5 above.

Nutritive value calculated for PITA PIZZA.

YIELD: 4 servings

Nutritive Values (per serving)		calories	48.3 kc
total fat	2.8 g	carbohydrates	2.0 g
monosaturated fat	0.9 g	fiber	0.0 g
polyunsaturated fat	0.2 g	protein	3.8 g
saturated fat	1.6 g	sodium	120.0 mg
cholesterol	8.3 mg	sugar	0.1 g

TORTILLA PIZZA

2   10-inch flour tortillas
    Olive oil spray
¾   cup FRESH TOMATO PIZZA SAUCE (Page 239) or commercial pizza sauce
⅓   cup sliced mushrooms
10 julienne strips of red, yellow or green bell pepper
4   teaspoons fresh grated Parmesan
4   ounces shredded part skim mozzarella cheese

1. Spray tortillas lightly on both sides with olive oil spray.

2. Spread one tortilla with 2 tablespoons of mozzarella; top with second tortilla.

3. Place on wire pizza frame or on cookie sheet. Bake in preheated 425° oven on next to bottom shelf of oven for 3 minutes; if tortilla puffs up, puncture with knife and press to deflate. Continue baking 2 minutes longer. Remove from oven and immediately roll lightly with rolling pin to flatten.

4. Spread tortilla with sauce: top with mushrooms and pepper strips. Sprinkle with Parmesan. Spray lightly with olive oil.

5. Bake in preheated 425° oven for 6 minutes; remove from oven and top with mozzarella. Return to oven for 3 minutes. Cut into 6-8 slices.

Since crust is not as firm as the traditional crust, you may wish to serve with plates and forks.

YIELD: 8 slices

Nutritive Values (per slice)		calories	93.4 kc
total fat	4.4 g	carbohydrates	8.0 g
monosaturated fat	1.4 g	fiber	0.0 g
polyunsaturated fat	0.4 g	protein	5.0 g
saturated fat	1.8 g	sodium	202.2 mg
cholesterol	8.9 mg	sugar	0.2 g

ENGLISH MUFFIN PIZZA

1 English muffin, sliced horizontally into thirds Olive oil spray 3 tablespoons pizza sauce (FRESH TOMATO PIZZA SAUCE, Page 239) or canned pizza sauce	Toppings of your choice (Pages 220, 221) ¼ teaspoon Parmesan ¼ cup (1 ounce) shredded part skim milk mozzarella

1. Spray top surface of each muffin slice lightly with olive oil.

2. Spread with 1 tablespoon pizza sauce.

3. Arrange assortment of toppings on sauce.

4. Sprinkle with Parmesan.

5. Spray lightly with olive oil.

6. Place muffins on foil-lined cookie sheet.

7. Bake 8-10 minutes on bottom shelf of preheated 475° oven. Block heat from above by placing large flat pan on top shelf of oven.

8. Remove from oven. Top with mozzarella and return to oven for 1-2 minutes until cheese melts.

Serve whole or cut in quarters with a kitchen scissors.

A few of these may be easily made in your toaster oven. For extra zip, add a pinch of red pepper flakes.

Nutritive analysis calculated for tomato and cheese topping only.

YIELD: 3 servings

Nutritive Values (per serving)		calories	88.1 kc
total fat	2.9 g	carbohydrates	11.3 g
monosaturated fat	1.0 g	fiber	0.0 g
polyunsaturated fat	0.3 g	protein	4.1 g
saturated fat	1.1 g	sodium	244.2 mg
cholesterol	5.5 mg	sugar	0.7 g

PIZZA LOAF

*1   18-inch loaf Italian or French bread
    Olive oil spray
6   ounces thinly sliced turkey breast, cut into strips

2½ cups prepared spaghetti sauce
6   ounces shredded part skim milk mozzarella
2   tablespoons freshly grated Parmesan

1. Cut loaf in half, lengthwise.

2. Pull dough from inside of each half loaf, leaving a ½-inch shell.

3. Spray loaf halves with olive oil inside and out. Place on a foil lined cookie sheet.

4. Bake 5-8 minutes in a preheated 400° oven. Take out before bread browns.

5. Combine spaghetti sauce and turkey.

6. Line inside of loaves with half of mozzarella. Pour in sauce mixture. Top with Parmesan.

7. Bake in preheated 400° oven for 15 minutes, adding remaining mozzarella for last 2-3 minutes. Take out of oven; cool 5 minutes. Cut in 1 inch slices.

*Buy bread from a good bakery!

To reduce sodium content, use low sodium spaghetti sauce and low sodium bread.

YIELD: 30 slices

Nutritive Values (per slice)			
total fat	1.3 g	calories	75.0 kc
monosaturated fat	0.4 g	carbohydrates	10.3 g
polyunsaturated fat	trace	fiber	0.7 g
saturated fat	0.7 g	protein	5.0 g
cholesterol	8.3 mg	sodium	237.5 mg
		sugar	0.7 g

SPINACH LINGUINI WITH EGGPLANT

3	cups peeled and diced eggplant	¼	teaspoon crushed red pepper flakes
½	teaspoon salt Water to cover eggplant	4	tablespoons chopped parsley (4 teaspoons dry)
2	tablespoons olive oil	8	ounces spinach linguini, cooked al dente and drained
2	cloves garlic, chopped		
½	cup chopped shallots	2	tablespoons Parmesan, freshly grated
1	28-ounce can Italian plum tomatoes and juice, coarsely chopped		

1. Soak eggplant in water and salt for a half hour. Rinse and drain thoroughly on paper towels

2. In large nonstick skillet or pan, sauté garlic, shallots and eggplant in olive oil for 10 minutes. Add tomatoes, pepper flakes and parsley; bring to boil and cook for 15 minutes or until desired consistency.

3. Mix boiling hot sauce with cooked pasta. Sprinkle with Parmesan. Prepare in advance through step 2 and refrigerate or freeze. Proceed with step 3 when ready to serve.

SPOTLIGHT *scintillates on spaghetti squash. Use as a spaghetti substitute or mix the strands of cooked spaghetti squash with the pasta itself and then add your sauce. Use half spaghetti squash and half pasta to reduce calories and increase fiber. The mixture will delight your calorie counters and pasta afficionados won't know the difference!*

YIELD: 10 servings

Nutritive Values (per serving)		calories	143.0 kc
total fat	3.8 g	carbohydrates	23.4 g
monosaturated fat	2.1 g	fiber	1.8 g
polyunsaturated fat	0.3 g	protein	4.7 g
saturated fat	3.8 g	sodium	270.0 mg
cholesterol	1.0 mg	sugar	3.3 g

LINGUINI

Serves 8 as an hors d'oeuvre

3	cloves garlic, chopped
2	teaspoons olive oil
8	cups Italian plum tomatoes, peeled, chopped and drained
½-1	teaspoon dried crushed pepper flakes
½	pound linguini (made without egg yolks)
2	tablespoons Parmesan
	Chopped parsley to garnish

1. Sauté garlic in olive oil in a nonstick skillet until wilted. Do not brown.

2. Add tomatoes and pepper flakes. Cook together, stirring occasionally until sauce thickens to desired consistency.

3. While sauce is cooking, prepare linguini according to package directions. Drain.

4. Add sauce to pasta.

5. Garnish with chopped parsley and Parmesan.

Prepare in advance through step 2; reheat before serving.

VARIATION: add 2 pounds cleaned *mussels to sauce during last 4 minutes of cooking time. One pound of crabmeat or mock crab may also be used. Add a few shrimp to make cholesterol watchers smile!

*SPOTLIGHT (Page 89)

YIELD: 8 servings

Nutritive Values (per serving)		calories	168.0 kc
total fat	2.6 g	carbohydrates	31.2 g
monosaturated fat	1.0 g	fiber	3.0 g
polyunsaturated fat	0.3 g	protein	6.3 g
saturated fat	0.5 g	sodium	49.0 mg
cholesterol	1.2 mg	sugar	5.5 g

10

TOP IT OFF LIGHTLY

sauces

RASPBERRY DIJON VINAIGRETTE

¼ cup raspberry vinegar
2 teaspoons fresh lemon juice
¼ cup each olive oil, walnut oil and corn or peanut oil
½ teaspoon salt
¼ teaspoon freshly ground pepper
1 teaspoon Dijon mustard

Combine and store in refrigerator in tightly covered jar.

To reduce sodium, use salt substitute.

YIELD: 1 cup

Nutritive Values (per tablespoon)		calories	30.3 kc
total fat	3.4 g	carbohydrates	0.3 g
monosaturated fat	0.0 g	fiber	0.1 g
polyunsaturated fat	0.3 g	protein	0.0 g
saturated fat	0.5 g	sodium	70.1 mg
cholesterol	0.0 mg	sugar	0.2 g

AVGOLEMONO SAUCE

Our adaptation of a Greek sauce, traditionally served with DOLMADES (Page 26), substituting monounsaturated olive oil for egg yolks.

1⅓ cups chicken broth or broth from DOLMADES (Page 26)
*2½ tablespoons instant blend flour
2 egg whites
4 teaspoons olive oil

¼ cup fresh lemon juice
¼ teaspoon salt
A few grinds of pepper
2 teaspoons chopped mint (optional)
A few drops yellow food coloring (optional)

1. Bring broth to boil; add flour, stirring to prevent lumps. Cook for one minute to thicken.

2. Place next 5 ingredients in food processor; process ½ minute; continue processing and pour in boiling hot stock gradually. Process 1 minute.

3. Stir in mint and yellow food coloring.

*SPOTLIGHT (Page 94)

May be made ahead and reheated in microwave or double boiler. Do not overheat!

YIELD: 1½ cups			
Nutritive Values (per tablespoon)		calories	14.0 kc
total fat	0.8 g	carbohydrates	1.0 g
monosaturated fat	0.6 g	fiber	trace
polyunsaturated fat	trace	protein	0.7 g
saturated fat	0.1 g	sodium	69.0 mg
cholesterol	trace	sugar	trace

MANGO CHUTNEY

1 cinnamon stick
2 teaspoons whole
   cloves
¼ teaspoon coriander
   seeds
2½ cups sugar
2 cups red wine vinegar
   Juice and grated rind
   of one lemon
1 teaspoon salt
3 cups chopped ripe
   mango

1 cup chopped Vidalia
   or sweet onion
½ cup dried currants
½ cup diced dates
⅛ teaspoon Tabasco
2 teaspoons curry
   powder
1 tablespoon mustard
   seed
¼ cup diced candied
   ginger

*1. Tie cinnamon stick, cloves and coriander seeds in a piece of cheesecloth. Place in 3 quart pot with next 4 ingredients. Bring to boil and continue boiling for 15 minutes.

2. Remove bag of spices and place remaining ingredients in pot. Bring to boil; reduce heat and simmer 1½-2 hours until thickened, stirring occasionally to prevent sticking.

3. Pour in sterile jars and store in refrigerator.

Use as condiment for curry dishes or with POACHED SALMON (Page 102) or JELLIED CHICKEN IN ASPIC (Page 30).

*SPOTLIGHT (Page 54)

YIELD: 3 cups

Nutritive Values (per tablespoon)		calories	62.6 kc
total fat	0.3 g	carbohydrates	16.8 g
monosaturated fat	0.0 g	fiber	0.6 g
polyunsaturated fat	0.0 g	protein	0.4 g
saturated fat	0.0 g	sodium	47.7 mg
cholesterol	0.0 mg	sugar	13.0 g

THOUSAND ISLAND DRESSING

½   cup lite mayonnaise
⅓   cup chili sauce
¼   cup sweet pickle
     relish, drained

¼   cup chopped green
     olives
1   hard boiled egg (white
     only), cubed

Combine all ingredients. Refrigerate in tightly covered jar.

OPTIONAL INGREDIENTS (add when ready to serve)
¼ cup diced jicama or Jerusalem artichoke
¼ cup diced water chestnuts

Use as a sauce for FISH TERRINE-21st CENTURY
(Page 108) and JELLIED CHICKEN IN ASPIC. (Page 30).

To reduce sodium content, omit olives and substitute low sodium
chili sauce. The fat and cholesterol content is lower than
mayonnaise alone because the recipe is stretched by the addition of
large amounts of fat and cholesterol free ingredients.

YIELD: 1 cup

Nutritive Values (per tablespoon)		calories	34.6 kc
total fat	2.4 g	carbohydrates	3.2 g
monosaturated fat	0.3 g	fiber	0.1 g
polyunsaturated fat	trace	protein	0.4 g
saturated fat	trace	sodium	172.9 mg
cholesterol	2.5 mg	sugar	0.0 g

FRESH TOMATO PIZZA SAUCE

*1   pound plum tomatoes (8 - 10), peeled, quartered and drained
¼   cup tomato paste
      Pinch sugar
      Dash Tabasco
½   teaspoon salt

2   teaspoons chopped fresh oregano (¾ teaspoon dried)
1   tablespoon chopped fresh basil (1 teaspoon dried)
**1   small clove garlic, peeled
1   tablespoon olive oil

Combine all ingredients in food processor. Blend with 4 on/off motions or until tomatoes are coarsely chopped. Do not overblend.

*SPOTLIGHT (Page 203)

**SPOTLIGHT (Page 66)

SPOTLIGHT *is a caution blinker on commercial pizza sauce. Read the label, giving attention to fat and sodium content. See SODIUM COMPARISON CHART (Page 141).*

YIELD: 2 cups

Nutritive Values (per tablespoon)		calories	8.9 kc
total fat	0.5 g	carbohydrates	1.2 g
monosaturated fat	0.3 g	fiber	0.3 g
polyunsaturated fat	0.1 g	protein	0.2 g
saturated fat	0.1 g	sodium	19.3 mg
cholesterol	0.0 mg	sugar	0.4 g

PLUM TOMATO SALSA

Crunchy and chunky and Cha Cha Cha

*2 cups diced plum tomatoes

1/3 cup each, cubed red, green and yellow peppers

1/2 cup diced jicama

1/2 cup diced Jerusalem artichoke

1 tablespoon minced shallots

1 clove minced garlic

2-4 teaspoons chopped chili peppers (optional)

1 tablespoon chopped cilantro or parsley

1 tablespoon tarragon vinegar

1 teaspoon garlic vinegar

1 tablespoon chopped fresh basil

1 tablespoon olive oil
A few drops of Tabasco (optional)

Combine above ingredients.

The vegetables and marinade may be prepared in advance. Combine an hour or two before serving.

*SPOTLIGHT (Page 203)

YIELD: 3 cups

Nutritive Values (per tablespoon)		calories	7.0 kc
total fat	0.3 g	carbohydrates	1.0 g
monosaturated fat	0.2 g	fiber	0.2 g
polyunsaturated fat	trace	protein	0.2 g
saturated fat	0.3 g	sodium	1.0 mg
cholesterol	0.0 mg	sugar	0.4 g

PESTO SUPREME

Not for the fainthearted! Make in summer using fresh basil.

2   **cups fresh basil leaves, tightly packed**
1/3   **cup fresh flat Italian parsley (any parsley will do)**
1/3   **cup olive oil**
4   **cloves garlic, minced**

1/3   **cup pignoli (pine nuts)**
1/2   **cup Parmesan, freshly grated**
1   **teaspoon freshly ground black pepper**
1/2   **cup low fat ricotta cheese**

1. Chop parsley and basil in food processor with 2 tablespoons olive oil and garlic. Blend until you have a green paste.

2. Add pine nuts and 2 tablespoons more of the olive oil. Blend two minutes. Add remaining ingredients and blend until smooth and well mixed.

Freezes well. Serve as a sauce for pasta. Warm but do not boil. Serve over fettuccini or cavatelli. Top with grated Romano. When using for pasta sauce, thin to desired consistency with 1-2 tablespoons water. A tablespoon added to minestrone greatly enhances the flavor.

Try PESTO SUPREME on pita. You'll love it!

PESTO PITA PIZZA (Page 227)

YIELD: 2 cups

Nutritive Values (per tablespoon)		calories	37.0 kc
total fat	3.3 g	carbohydrates	0.7 g
monosaturated fat	2.6 g	fiber	trace
polyunsaturated fat	0.3 g	protein	1.3 g
saturated fat	0.9 g	sodium	34.2 mg
cholesterol	2.4 mg	sugar	0.1 g

COCKTAIL SAUCE

1 cup chili sauce
1-3 tablespoons horseradish
2 tablespoons sweet pickle relish
1 teaspoon Worcestershire sauce
$^1/_8$ teaspoon Tabasco
6 seedless green olives
2 tablespoons capers

3-4 tablespoons lemon juice
1 teaspoon chopped parsley
$^1/_4$ teaspoon each: dill weed, celery salt, paprika, lemon pepper, salt and freshly ground pepper

Chop all ingredients in food processor with steel blade.

Store in refrigerator in covered container.

SPOTLIGHT *suggests avoiding salty seasonings: soy sauce, tamari, maggi, barbeque squce, herbed and seasoned salts, dry soup mixes, canned soups and bouillon cubes. Use instead: salt-free mustard, catsup, onion or garlic powder, citrus juice, wine, vinegar , fresh grated ginger and other fresh herbs. Variety is the spice of life!*

To reduce sodium content use low sodium chili sauce, horseradish, seasoned salt, and pickle relish. Omit capers and olives.

YIELD: 1$^1/_2$ cups

Nutritive Values (per tablespoon)		calories	15.4 kc
total fat	0.1 g	carbohydrates	3.6 g
monosaturated fat	0.1 g	fiber	trace g
polyunsaturated fat	trace	protein	0.3 g
saturated fat	trace	sodium	225.0 mg
cholesterol	0.0 mg	sugar	0.1 g

CUCUMBER DILL SAUCE

½ onion chopped
*3 cups low fat yogurt,
 drained 4 hours

**2 teaspoons lemon juice
1 small cucumber,
 peeled and chopped
1 sprig dill for garnish

Mix all ingredients well; refrigerate and garnish with one dill sprig. If your diet allows, replace some of the yogurt with mayonnaise.

*ALL ABOUT YOGURT (Page 154)

**SPOTLIGHT (Page 49)

SPOTLIGHT *circles the popular gourmet cucumber that requires no peeling. (Waxed cucumbers need to be peeled.) To remove seeds, cut cucumber in half lengthwise and scoop out seeds with a teaspoon. Color and crispness combine in the cucumber.*

YIELD: 2½ cups

Nutritive Values (per tablespoon)		calories	12.5 kc
total fat	trace	carbohydrates	1.6 g
monosaturated fat	0.1 g	fiber	0.2 g
polyunsaturated fat	trace	protein	1.0 g
saturated fat	0.2 g	sodium	12.1 mg
cholesterol	1.1 mg	sugar	1.0 g

FRUITED YOGURT SAUCE

*1½ cups low fat yogurt,
    drained 6-8 hours
2-4 tablespoons sugar free
    Red Raspberry Fruit
    Spread

2   teaspoons lime juice
½   teaspoon grated lime
    rind
1-2 teaspoons finely
    chopped candied
    ginger (optional)

Combine and serve as sauce for dipping fruit.

*ALL ABOUT YOGURT (Page 154)

YIELD: 1 cup

Nutritive Values (per tablespoon)		calories	15.8 kc
total fat	0.4 g	carbohydrates	2.1 g
monosaturated fat	0.1 g	fiber	0.1 g
polyunsaturated fat	0.0 g	protein	1.2 g
saturated fat	0.2 g	sodium	15.0 mg
cholesterol	1.3 mg	sugar	1.3 g

SALMON SAUCE

1   6½-ounce can red
    salmon, drained
1   shallot, skinned and
    quartered
2   tablespoons fresh
    lemon juice
½   cup lite mayonnaise

*1   cup low fat yogurt,
     drained 2 hours
½   teaspoon paprika
3   anchovies (optional)
2   tablespoons dill weed
    (2 teaspoons dried)

1. Chop all ingredients in food processor with steel knife.

2. Chill before serving.

*ALL ABOUT YOGURT (Page 154)

SUGGESTION

Serve with JELLIED CHICKEN IN ASPIC (page 30).

Nutritive analysis reflects the use of 3 anchovies which is 25% of the sodium content.

YIELD: 2 cups

Nutritive Values (per tablespoon)		calories	30.0 kc
total fat	2.1 g	carbohydrates	1.2 g
monosaturated fat	0.5 g	fiber	trace g
polyunsaturated fat	1.1 g	protein	1.5 g
saturated fat	0.4 g	sodium	49.4 mg
cholesterol	0.4 mg	sugar	0.4 g

LOBSTER SAUCE

¾ cup skim milk	½-1 teaspooon Dijon mustard
¾ cup dry white wine	
1 tablespoon margarine	*3 tablespoons instant blend flour
¼ teaspoon salt	
⅛ teaspoon freshly ground pepper	**⅓ cup finely chopped lobster or crab (real or mock)
¼ teaspoon paprika	1 tablespoon Parmesan

1. Combine first 7 ingredients in sauce pan. Heat to boiling over medium heat. Add flour, stirring to prevent lumps and continue cooking for 2 minutes.

2. Add lobster or crab and Parmesan and cook until heated through.

*SPOTLIGHT (Page 94)

**SPOTLIGHT (Pages 95, 105)

Make in advance; cover closely with plastic wrap and refrigerate. Reheat when ready to serve.

Nutritive values calculated with mock crab.

YIELD: 2 cups

Nutritive Values (per tablespoon)		calories	15.0 kc
total fat	0.5 g	carbohydrates	1.1 g
monosaturated fat	0.1 g	fiber	trace
polyunsaturated fat	0.2 g	protein	0.7 g
saturated fat	trace	sodium	55.0 mg
cholesterol	0.7 mg	sugar	0.3 g

11
SNACKS, CRACKS,
AND BREADS

SNACKOS

½	cup margarine	1	teaspoon celery salt
2	teaspoons Worcestershire sauce	½	teaspoon Tabasco
		*4	quarts dry cereal
1	teaspoon seasoned salt	1	10-ounce box thin pretzels
1	teaspoon garlic salt	1	pound (4 cups) unsalted nuts (walnuts, almonds, peanuts)

1. Melt margarine; add seasonings.

2. Mix cereals and nuts in large roaster pan. Pour seasoned margarine over cereal mixture. Mix to coat well.

3. Bake at 200° for 1 hour, stirring occasionally.

*Use cereals like Cheerios, Wheat Chex, Rice Chex, Corn Chex, spoon-size Shredded Wheat, etc.

SPOTLIGHT *is a night light on SNACKOS when it leads the way to breakfast cereals served during the cocktail hour. They are high in fiber, low in fats and cholesterol. Don't forget to read the labels.*

Nutrient values based on spoon-size Shredded Wheat and Rice Chex. To reduce fat and calories, use ¼ cup margarine. To reduce sodium, use salt-free herb seasonings and salt-free thin pretzels.

YIELD: 32 ½-cup servings

Nutritive Values (per serving)			
total fat	15.1 g	calories	410.0 kc
monosaturated fat	5.9 g	carbohydrates	61.5 g
polyunsaturated fat	6.1 g	fiber	6.9 g
saturated fat	1.4 g	protein	12.4 g
cholesterol	0.0 mg	sodium	370.5 mg
		sugar	1.4 g

ROCK & ROLL POPCORN

⅓	cup popcorn, dry popped	1	teaspoon Worcestershire sauce
1	tablespoon margarine, melted	½	teaspoon garlic salt
1	tablespoon dried dill weed	½	teaspoon onion powder
*1	teaspoon lemon pepper		

1. Prepare popcorn.

2. Combine remaining ingredients and toss with popcorn.

3. Spread on jelly roll pan.

4. Bake in 250° oven 6-8 minutes.

*LOW SODIUM LEMON PEPPER (Page 140)

SPOTLIGHT *is turned on by dry popped popcorn, a low fat, high fiber snack. It's what we put on the popcorn that makes it unhealthful. You'll pop your lid for popcorn!*

YIELD: 6 servings

Nutritive Values (per serving)			
total fat	1.9 g	calories	34.0 kc
monosaturated fat	0.6 g	carbohydrates	3.5 g
polyunsaturated fat	1.1 g	fiber	0.4 g
saturated fat	0.2 g	protein	0.7 g
cholesterol	0.0 mg	sodium	34.7 mg
		sugar	0.1 g

NUT ZINGERS

Used in moderation, dry roasted almonds, walnuts and peanuts are an excellent source of protein, minerals and fiber. Besides providing good nutrition, nuts are a tasty way to add decorating highlights and crunch. Always keep in mind that nuts are high in fat content and calories. See comparison chart at bottom of page.

2	teaspoons ginger	2	tablespoons melted margarine
½	teaspoon allspice	½	teaspoon seasoned salt
1	pound walnut halves or whole blanched almonds		

1. Boil nuts and spices for 3 minutes in water to cover; drain.

2. Spread on greased pan. Bake at 350° for 15 minutes, turning once after 8 minutes. Toss with margarine and seasoned salt. Return to oven for 5 minutes.

Nutritive values calculated using walnuts.

YIELD: 4 cups

Nutritive Values (per ¼ cup)		calories	206.1 kc
total fat	20.0 g	carbohydrates	5.7 g
monosaturated fat	4.8 g	fiber	1.4 g
polyunsaturated fat	12.4 g	protein	4.3 g
saturated fat	1.9 g	sodium	89.0 mg
cholesterol	0.0 mg	sugar	0.6 g

COMPARISON CHART: DRY ROASTED NUTS

	Almonds ¼ cup	Cashews ¼ cup	Hazel Nut ¼ cup	Pecans ¼ cup	Walnuts (English) ¼ cup	Peanuts ¼ cup
g fat	15.0	15.9	18.0	18.2	18.5	18.0
g mono	9.7	9.3	14.1	11.4	4.2	8.9
g poly	3.1	2.7	1.7	4.5	11.7	5.7
g sat	1.4	3.1	1.3	1.5	1.7	2.5
mg chol	0.0	0.0	0.0	0.0	0.0	0.0
g carb	5.9	11.2	4.4	5.0	5.5	5.9
g fiber	2.7	2.5	2.4	2.1	1.4	2.9
g protein	5.7	5.2	3.7	2.1	4.3	9.4
mg sodium	3.2	5.2	0.7	0.2	3.0	5.8
g sugar	1.6	2.1	1.3	1.2	0.6	1.6
kc calories	169.3	196.8	181.7	180.3	192.5	207.0

CROUTONS

Bread
Butter flavored oil spray
Seasoned salt

1. Spray bread slices lightly with butter flavored vegetable oil spray or brush with melted margarine.

2. Sprinkle lightly with seasoned salt. Cut into cubes.

3. Spread out on flat pan in single layer.

4. Bake at 250° for 20 minutes or until dried, turning after 10 minutes.

Nutritive values will vary according to choice of bread.

CROUSTADES

Keep a supply of these in your freezer for unexpected guests.

36 slices fresh thin sliced bread
¼ cup margarine

1. Cut a round from the center of each slice of bread with a 2½ inch cookie cutter, or the rim of a glass.

2. Coat miniature muffin tins with margarine or vegetable spray.

3. Carefully fit the bread rounds into the muffin tins, pushing the center of the bread into bottom and gently molding the round onto the sides with fingertips. Each should form a perfect cup.

4. Bake for 8-12 minutes at 325° or until golden brown; remove from the tins and cool.

Fill with mushroom, chicken or seafood filling.

See FILLINGS in index.

Nutrient values will vary according to choice of filling and bread. Vegetable oil spray further reduces fat and cholesterol.

MELBA TOAST

1　**loaf unsliced bread**
　Butter flavored oil spray
　Seasoned salt (optional)

1. Freeze bread.

2. Cut crust off one end; discard crust.

3. Spray end of loaf lightly with oil spray.

4. Cut off thin slice.

5. Continue spraying end and cutting off slices until loaf is used.

6. Lay slices on cookie sheet.

7. Bake at 250° until dried out and lightly browned.

For a zesty flavor, sprinkle very lightly with seasoned salt.

The nutrient values will vary according to type of bread and the amount of oil spray and salt used. To reduce sodium use salt substitute and low sodium bread.

YIELD: 8 servings

Nutritive Values (per serving)		calories	81.0 kc
total fat	5.0 g	carbohydrates	6.0 g
monosaturated fat	1.0 g	fiber	7.0 g
polyunsaturated fat	7.0 f	protein	2.0 g
saturated fat	0.6 g	sodium	664.0 mg
cholesterol	4.0 mg	sugar	3.0 g

WHOLE WHEAT SESAME CRISPS

¾ cup whole wheat flour
¾ cup all purpose flour
¾ teaspoon salt
¼ teaspoon baking soda
2 teaspoons brown sugar

3 tablespoons oil
4-5 tablespoons water
2 tablespoons sesame seeds
Vegetable oil spray

1. Place first five ingredients in food processor with plastic blade; process with 1 on/off motion. Add oil and process ½ minute. Pour water through feed tube 1 tablespoon at a time, until the dough looks crumbly, but will hold its shape when pressed into a ball. Add sesame seeds and process with 2 on/off motions.

2. Roll dough with rolling pin into a paper-thin sheet. Cut into desired shapes and place on greased baking sheet. Spray tops with oil.

3. Bake in preheated 400° oven for 7-10 minutes or until nicely browned.

Store in tightly covered container to preserve crispness.

VARIATION: CARAWAY RYE CRISPS:
Substitute ¾ cup rye flour for the whole wheat flour and 2 tablespoons caraway seeds for the sesame seeds.

YIELD: 60 small pieces

Nutritive Values (per piece)		calories	19.0 kc
total fat	0.9 g	carbohydrates	2.4 g
monosaturated fat	0.4 g	fiber	0.3 g
polyunsaturated fat	0.3 g	protein	0.4 g
saturated fat	0.1 g	sodium	35.7 mg
cholesterol	0.0 mg	sugar	0.2 g

TORTILLA CRAX

Flour tortillas, any size.
Vegetable oil spray

1. Spray both sides lightly with olive or corn oil.

2. Sprinkle one side with your choice of seasonings:
   seasoned salt, lemon pepper, sesame or poppy seeds,
   garlic salt (use sparingly), dill weed, Parmesan.

3. Bake at 425° on oil sprayed cookie sheet or foil for
   3-4 minutes or until lightly browned.

Cut into pieces with scissors (while still hot) or serve whole
and let guests break off pieces.

SPOTLIGHT beams on commercial herb mixtures and salt free seasonings which you will find on your grocery shelves. They are available in various combinations of spices and flavors. Keep a variety on hand.

PITA TRIANGLES

A delicious munchy cracker for good eating as is — or with a dip.

1. Separate pita bread into two thin discs by cutting around
   edge with scissors or sharp knife.

2. Spray with olive or vegetable oil.

3. Sprinkle with your choice of: seasoned salt, lemon
   pepper, sesame or poppy seeds, garlic salt (use
   sparingly), dill weed, Parmesan.

4. Cut into triangles.

5. Bake in preheated 375° oven for 7-8 minutes or until
   lightly browned.

Nutritive values for CRAX and TRIANGLES vary with size and
choice and amount of seasonings.

BEER BREAD

This is good with pasta. Make a double measure and keep a loaf in your freezer.

3	cups self-rising flour
3	tablespoons sugar
1	12-ounce can beer, room temperature
1	egg white, beaten with 1 teaspoon water
	Poppy seeds or sesame seeds

1. Mix all ingredients together.

2. Brush with beaten egg whites and sprinkle with poppy seeds or sesame seeds.

3. Bake at 375° for 45 minutes in a greased 9 × 5 inch loaf pan.

Use leftover BEER BREAD slices in making MELBA TOAST (Page 253). The sugar in the beer carmelizes as the bread toasts.

YIELD: 20 slices

Nutritive Values (per slice)		calories	81.0 kc
total fat	0.2 g	carbohydrates	16.6 g
monosaturated fat	0.0 g	fiber	0.5 g
polyunsaturated fat	0.0 g	protein	1.9 g
saturated fat	trace	sodium	203.4 mg
cholesterol	0.0 mg	sugar	2.0 g

 CORNY CORN MUFFINS

We've added corn to corn muffins!

2 egg whites	⅔ cup corn meal
¼ teaspoon salt	3 tablespoons oil
2 teaspoons baking powder	1 14½-ounce can cream-style corn
2 tablespoons sugar	¾ cup whole kernel corn, well drained
1⅓ cups sifted all purpose flour	

1. Beat egg whites, salt, baking powder and sugar until stiff.

2. Stir in flour and cornmeal alternately with oil and corn, mixing just enough to blend. Do not overmix.

3. Grease muffin tins or cornstick pans; fill ⅔ full. Bake in preheated 425° oven for 20-24 minutes or until they test dry with toothpick.

Add 1 4-ounce can chilies, drained, for a zippy version!

VARIATION: Use 9 ounce box of corn bread (muffin) mix. Follow the directions on the package, substituting an equal amount of cream-style corn for the liquid (water or milk) and adding ¾ cup of well drained whole kernel corn.

For a sweet finish, spread with HONEY BUTTER.

HONEY BUTTER

½ pound tub margarine	
¼ cup honey	

Mix margarine and honey until well blended. Refrigerate in a covered container.

Nutritive values of muffins calculated without HONEY BUTTER.

YIELD: 18 muffins

Nutritive Values (per muffin)		calories	98.0 kc
total fat	2.5 g	carbohydrates	17.2 g
monosaturated fat	1.0 g	fiber	1.6 g
polyunsaturated fat	0.8 g	protein	2.4 g
saturated fat	0.4 g	sodium	131.5 mg
cholesterol	0.0 mg	sugar	1.0 g

FILLED PARTY LOAVES

Crusty round French breads, round pumpernickels or long rye breads, hollowed out, make great containers for dips. The loaf can be refilled when dip is used up. The bread is particularly delicious when soaked up with the dip. The loaf itself can be cut into chunks.

1. To prepare loaf: Cut ¾ inch slice off top of loaf. Cut or scoop out soft bread, leaving at least ¼ inch shell. Cut top slice and scooped out bread into cubes to use for dipping. (Wrap to prevent drying out.)

2. Place loaf on serving platter and fill loaf with desired dip. Garnish with parsley or paprika as desired. Place cubes of bread around loaf.

Loaf may be prepared ahead of time and stored in plastic bag in freezer or refrigerator.

SUGGESTED COMBINATIONS

PUMPERNICKEL BREAD:

HUMMUS BI TAHINI (Page 149)

HERRING SPREAD (Page 168)

GREAT GARBANZO DIP (Page 147)

GEFILTE FISH DIP (Page 167)

FRENCH OR VIENNA BREAD:

ARTICHOKE SMOOTHY (Page 165)

CURRY DIP (Page 161)

GARDEN DELIGHT (Page 164)

CRABMEAT FLORIDA (Page 115)

INDEX

ORDER FORM

Please mail all orders and checks to: ROCKDALE RIDGE PRESS
P.O. Box 37848
Cincinnati, Ohio 45222
513-891-9900

Please send _______ copies of **BEGINNING LIGHT**   at $12.95
    plus 71¢ tax, $2.00 handling
Please send _______ copies of **IN THE BEGINNING**   at $10.95
    plus 60¢ tax, $2.00 handling
Please send _______ copies of **BEGINNING AGAIN**   at $10.95
    plus 60¢ tax, $2.00 handling

Enclosed is my check .... Total $ _______

Name ________________________________ Phone ____________

Address ____

City ____________________ State _________ Zip ____________

Gift card message ______________________________________

____

____

- -

Please send _______ copies of **BEGINNING LIGHT**   at $12.95
    plus 71¢ tax, $2.00 handling
Please send _______ copies of **IN THE BEGINNING**   at $10.95
    plus 60¢ tax, $2.00 handling
Please send _______ copies of **BEGINNING AGAIN**   at $10.95
    plus 60¢ tax, $2.00 handling

Enclosed is my check .... Total $ _______

Name ________________________________ Phone ____________

Address ____

City ____________________ State _________ Zip ____________

Gift card message ______________________________________

____

____

- -

Please send _______ copies of **BEGINNING LIGHT**   at $12.95
    plus 71¢ tax, $2.00 handling
Please send _______ copies of **IN THE BEGINNING**   at $10.95
    plus 60¢ tax, $2.00 handling
Please send _______ copies of **BEGINNING AGAIN**   at $10.95
    plus 60¢ tax, $2.00 handling

Enclosed is my check .... Total $ _______

Name ________________________________ Phone ____________

Address ____

City ____________________ State _________ Zip ____________

Gift card message ______________________________________

____

____

ACKNOWLEDGEMENTS

The editors of **BEGINNING LIGHT** gratefully acknowledge the following as sources of data and background information:

American Seafood Institute Report

American Soybean Association

Beef Board of Ohio

California Artichoke Advisory Board

Toni Cashnelli, The Cincinnati Enquirer

Dairy Nutrition Council, Inc.

Dannon Yogurt

DIET SIMPLE PLUS™ Computer program

Idaho-Washington Dry Pea & Lentil Commission

Hillshire Farm & Kahn's

Louis Kemp Seafood Co.

Ellen Kleinfeld, R.D., L.D.

The Kroger Company

The Beef Industry Council and The Pork Industry Group of The National Live Stock and Meat Board

National Broiler Council

National Turkey Federation

Nutritive Value of American Foods No. 456, USDA

Ohio State Extension Service

Reynolds Metals Co.

Joyce Rosencrans, The Cincinnati Post

Saco Foods, Inc.

Diane Schneider, R.D., L.D.

U.S. Department of Health and Human Services

NOTES

NOTES

TWO MORE WINNERS!

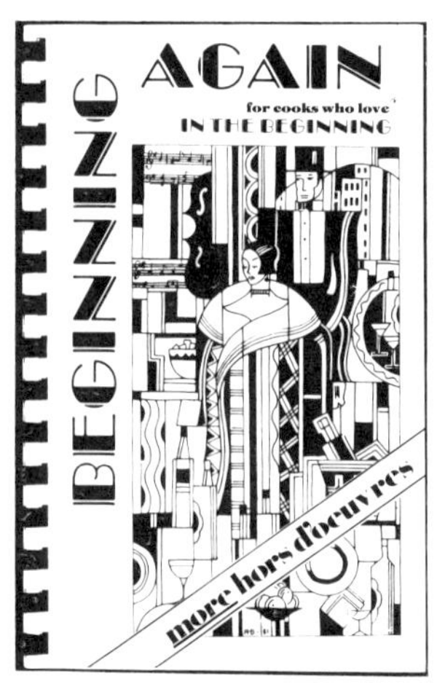

If you are enjoying your copy of BEGINNING LIGHT, you will love
IN THE BEGINNING and BEGINNING AGAIN, our other
nationally acclaimed hors d'oeuvres cookbooks. With all three books
in your kitchen you will own the most comprehensive collection of
hors d'oeuvres recipes in print.

ORDER FORM

Please mail all orders and checks to: ROCKDALE RIDGE PRESS
P.O. Box 37848
Cincinnati, Ohio 45222
513-891-9900

Please send _______ copies of **BEGINNING LIGHT**   at $12.95
plus 71¢ tax, $2.00 handling
Please send _______ copies of **IN THE BEGINNING**   at $10.95
plus 60¢ tax, $2.00 handling
Please send _______ copies of **BEGINNING AGAIN**   at $10.95
plus 60¢ tax, $2.00 handling

Enclosed is my check . . . . Total $ _______

Name _______________________________ Phone _______

Address ____

City _______________________ State _________ Zip _______

Gift card message _____________________________________

____

· ·

Please send _______ copies of **BEGINNING LIGHT**   at $12.95
plus 71¢ tax, $2.00 handling
Please send _______ copies of **IN THE BEGINNING**   at $10.95
plus 60¢ tax, $2.00 handling
Please send _______ copies of **BEGINNING AGAIN**   at $10.95
plus 60¢ tax, $2.00 handling

Enclosed is my check . . . . Total $ _______

Name _______________________________ Phone _______

Address ____

City _______________________ State _________ Zip _______

Gift card message _____________________________________

____

· ·

Please send _______ copies of **BEGINNING LIGHT**   at $12.95
plus 71¢ tax, $2.00 handling
Please send _______ copies of **IN THE BEGINNING**   at $10.95
plus 60¢ tax, $2.00 handling
Please send _______ copies of **BEGINNING AGAIN**   at $10.95
plus 60¢ tax, $2.00 handling

Enclosed is my check . . . . Total $ _______

Name _______________________________ Phone _______

Address ____

City _______________________ State _________ Zip _______

Gift card message _____________________________________

____